BIG IDEAS
MATH®
Integrated Mathematics III

Student Journal

- Maintaining Mathematical Proficiency

- Exploration Journal

- Notetaking with Vocabulary

- Extra Practice

BIG IDEAS
LEARNING®

Erie, Pennsylvania

Photo Credits

Cover Image Mix3r/Shutterstock.com

7 *top left* Mega Pixel/Shutterstock.com;
top right JIANG HONGYAN/Shutterstock.com;
bottom left forest_strider/Shutterstock.com;
bottom right Mario Savoia/Shutterstock.com;
12 *top left* Coprid/Shutterstock.com;
top right HomeArt/Shutterstock.com;
bottom left Svetlana Foote/Shutterstock.com;
bottom right indigolotos/Shutterstock.com;
13 PaulPaladin/Shutterstock.com;
279 Skylines/Shutterstock.com;
286 Denis Cristo/Shutterstock.com;
289 sauletas/Shutterstock.com

Printed in the United States

ISBN 13: 978-1-68033-090-8
ISBN 10: 1-68033-090-X

89101112-VLP-20 19 18

Contents

Contents

Contents

Contents

Contents

Contents

About the Student Journal

Maintaining Mathematical Proficiency

The Maintaining Mathematical Proficiency corresponds to the Pupil Edition Chapter Opener. Here you have the opportunity to practice prior skills necessary to move forward.

Exploration Journal

The Exploration pages correspond to the Explorations and accompanying exercises in the Pupil Edition. Here you have room to show your work and record your answers.

Notetaking with Vocabulary

This student-friendly notetaking component is designed to be a reference for key vocabulary, properties, and core concepts from the lesson. There is room to add definitions in your words and take notes about the core concepts.

Extra Practice

Each section of the Pupil Edition has an additional Practice with room for you to show your work and record your answers.

Chapter 1 Maintaining Mathematical Proficiency

Find the area of the circle or regular polygon.

1.

4.7 in.

2.

3.7 ft

5 ft

3. a circle with a diameter of 74.6 centimeters

4. a regular hexagon with a perimeter of 42 yards and an apothem of 4.25 yards

5. a circle with a circumference of 24π meters

Find the surface area and volume of the solid.

6.

8 in.

6 in.

12 in.

7.

35 cm

28 cm

8.

58 yd

9.

37 m

23 m

Name _____ Date _____

1.1 Modeling with Area
For use with Exploration 1.1

Essential Question How can you use the population and area of a region to describe how densely the region is populated?

1 **EXPLORATION:** Exploring Population and Area

Work with a partner. Use the Internet to find the population and land area of each county in California. Then find the number of people per square mile for each county.

a. Mendocino County

b. Lake County

c. Yolo County

d. Napa County

e. Sonoma County

f. Marin County

1.1 **Modeling with Area** (continued)

---

2 **EXPLORATION:** Analyzing Population and Area

Work with a partner. The six counties in Exploration 1 appear on a map as shown.

a. Without calculating, how would you expect the number of people per square mile in the entire 6-county region to compare to the values for each individual county in Exploration 1?

b. Use the populations and land areas in Exploration 1 to justify your answer in part (a).

Communicate Your Answer

3. How can you use the population and area of a region to describe how densely the region is populated?

4. Find the population and land area of the county in which you live. How densely populated is your county compared to the counties in Exploration 1?

5. In Exploration 1, the two northern counties are less densely populated than the other four. What factors do you think might influence how densely a region is populated?

1.1 Notetaking with Vocabulary
For use after Lesson 1.1

In your own words, write the meaning of each vocabulary term.

population density

Notes:

1.1 **Notetaking with Vocabulary** (continued)

Extra Practice

1. About 70,000 people live in a circular region with a 30-mile radius. Find the population density in people per square mile.

2. About 370,000 people live in a circular region with a 5-mile radius. Find the population density in people per square mile.

3. A map of the state of Montana is approximately rectangular with a length of 590 miles and a width of 250 miles.

   a. Montana has a population of about 990,000. Find the population density in people per square mile.

   b. The table shows the estimated populations for domestic sheep and cattle in Montana. Find the population density in animals per square mile for each animal.

Animal	Sheep	Cattle
Population	225,000	2.6 million

4. About 860,000 people live in a circular region with a population density of about 6480 people per square mile. Find the radius of the region.

1.1 **Notetaking with Vocabulary** (continued)

5. You have 350 yards of fencing to build a rectangular corral of length ℓ and width w.

   a. Write an expression that represents the area of the corral in terms of ℓ.

   b. Use your expression from part (a) to determine the dimensions of the corral that maximize the area.

In Exercises 6 and 7, describe how the change affects the surface area of the right prism or cylinder.

6. doubling all linear dimensions

8 ft

3 ft

7. multiplying the height by 4

5 ft

5 ft

13 ft

8. You are wrapping a birthday present that is a rectangular prism. The present is 26 inches long, 12 inches tall, and 20 inches wide.

   a. What is the minimum area of wrapping paper required to cover the box?

   b. What is the minimum area of wrapping paper required if you place an identical box on top of the original and wrap them together?

   c. Should you cut your wrapping paper to the minimum area you found in parts (a) and (b)? Explain.

1.2 Modeling with Volume
For use with Exploration 1.2

Essential Question   How can you use the mass and volume of an object to describe the density of the object?

---

1   EXPLORATION: Finding Densities

Work with a partner. Approximate the volume of each object whose mass is given. Then find the mass per unit of volume, or *density*, of each object.

a. Brick: 2.3 kg

5.7 cm

20 cm   10 cm

b. Log: 18.1 kg

44 cm

├─28 cm─┤

c. Golf ball: 45.9 g

├────── 43 mm ──────┤

d. Cork: 2.6 g

├──── 3 cm ────┤

3 cm

├─ 1.5 cm ─┤

1.2 **Modeling with Volume** (continued)

2 **EXPLORATION:** Analyzing Densities

Work with a partner. The objects in Exploration 1 with a density greater than 1 gram per cubic centimeter will sink in water. The objects with a density less than 1 gram per cubic centimeter will float in water. You place each object in Exploration 1 in a bucket of water.

   a. Which object(s) sink? Justify your answer.

   b. Would your answer in part (a) change when each object is cut in half and placed in water? Explain your reasoning.

   c. You dissolve enough salt in a bucket of water to cause one of the sunken objects to float. Which object is it and why do you think this happens?

Communicate Your Answer

   3. How can you use the mass and volume of an object to describe the density of the object?

   4. Use the Internet or some other reference to research the densities of water, mineral oil, and beeswax. You combine these substances in a bucket. How do you think the liquids interact? Where would the beeswax settle?

Name_____ Date_____

1.2 Notetaking with Vocabulary
For use after Lesson 1.2

In your own words, write the meaning of each vocabulary term.

density

Notes:

1.2 **Notetaking with Vocabulary** (continued)

Extra Practice

1. The density of a feather is about 0.0025 gram per cubic centimeter and the density of a brick is about 1.84 grams per cubic centimeter. You have 1000 grams of feathers and 1000 grams of bricks. What volume of each do you have?

2. Before 1965, dimes and quarters were made of silver. The density of silver is about 10.5 grams per cubic centimeter. Find the mass of the coins given their dimensions.

   a. Dime: 1.79 centimeters diameter, 0.135 centimeter thickness

   b. Quarter: 2.43 centimeters diameter, 0.175 centimeter thickness

3. A tree harvester estimates the height of a white pine trunk to have a height of about 22 meters and a base diameter of about 0.75 meter.

   a. The wood has a density of 425 kilograms per cubic meter. Find the mass of the trunk to the nearest kilogram.

   b. The tree puts on a growth ring of 8 millimeters and its height increases by 1 meter this year. How many cubic meters of wood does the tree trunk produce after one year?

   c. The tree grows at a constant rate. Compare the amount of growth this year to the amount of growth 3 years from now.

1.2 **Notetaking with Vocabulary** (continued)

In Exercises 4 and 5, describe how the change affects the volume of the prism or cylinder.

4. multiplying the radius by 5

2 ft

6 ft

5. multiplying the length and width by $\frac{1}{6}$

3 cm

12 cm

18 cm

6. A conical pile of sand has a diameter of 175 feet and a slant height of 100 feet. After one day, the linear dimensions are $\frac{2}{3}$ of the original dimensions.

   a. How does this change affect the volume of the pile?

   b. It takes about 200 pounds of sand to fill a traditional sand box. How many sand boxes can be filled with the remaining sand? A cubic foot of sand weighs about 125 pounds.

1.3 Cross Sections of Solids
For use with Exploration 1.3

Essential Question   How can you use a piece of food to create a real-life cross section?

Imagine cutting through a piece of food. The intersection formed by the cut you make and the piece of food is called a **cross section**. The shape of the cross section depends on the angle of the cut you make.

1   EXPLORATION: Describing Cross Sections

Work with a partner. Describe the shapes of the cross sections that are formed by making cuts into each given food so that it is separated into two congruent parts.

a. wheel of cheese

b. watermelon

c. stick of butter

d. cucumber

1.3 **Cross Sections of Solids** (continued)

2 **EXPLORATION:** Forming Cross Sections

Work with a partner. Describe how you can slice the portion
of cheese so that the cross section formed is the given shape.

  a. triangle

  b. rectangle

  c. trapezoid

Communicate Your Answer

  3. How can you use a piece of food to create a real-life cross section?

  4. Is there more than one way to slice the portion of cheese in Exploration 2 to form
     a triangular cross section? Explain. Use drawings to support your answer.

1.3 Notetaking with Vocabulary
For use after Lesson 1.3

In your own words, write the meaning of each vocabulary term.

cross section

Notes:

1.3   Notetaking with Vocabulary (continued)

Extra Practice

In Exercises 1–4, describe the cross section formed by the intersection of the plane and the solid.

1.

2.

3.

4.

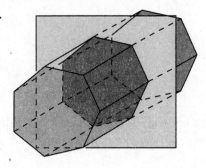

1.3 **Notetaking with Vocabulary** (continued)

In Exercises 5 and 6, draw the cross section formed by the described plane that contains $\overline{AB}$. What is the shape of the cross section?

5. plane is perpendicular to base

6. plane is perpendicular to bottom face

7. You have a pie with a radius of 4.5 inches and a height of 2.25 inches. You cut the pie vertically to make two congruent parts.

   a. Find the perimeter and area of the cross section formed by the cut.

   b. If you cut one half of the pie again vertically to make two congruent parts, what is the perimeter and area of this new cross section formed?

Name_____ Date_____

Essential Question How can you create a solid of revolution?

A **solid of revolution** is a three-dimensional figure that is formed by rotating a two-dimensional shape around an axis.

---

1 **EXPLORATION:** Creating Solids of Revolution

Go to *BigIdeasMath.com* for an interactive tool to investigate this exploration.

Work with a partner. Tape the 5-inch side of a 3-inch by 5-inch index card to a pencil, as shown.

3 in.

5 in.

   a. Rotate the pencil. What type of solid is produced by the rotating index card? What are its dimensions?

   b. Tape the 3-inch side of the index card to the pencil. Rotate the pencil. What type of solid is produced by the rotating index card? What are its dimensions?

3 in.

5 in.

   c. Do the solids in parts (a) and (b) have the same surface area? the same volume? Justify your answers.

   d. Cut the index card in half along its diagonal. Tape the 5-inch leg of the triangle formed to a pencil. Rotate the pencil. What type of solid is produced? What are its dimensions?

   e. Tape the 3-inch leg to a pencil. Rotate the pencil. What type of solid is produced? What are its dimensions?

   f. Do the solids in parts (d) and (e) have the same surface area? the same volume? Justify your answers.

1.4 **Solids of Revolution** (continued)

---

2 **EXPLORATION:** Creating Solids of Revolution

Go to *BigIdeasMath.com* for an interactive tool to investigate this exploration.

Work with a partner. Tape the straight side of a protractor, similar to the one at the right, to a pencil, as shown.

    a. Rotate the pencil. What type of solid is produced by the rotating protractor? What are its dimensions?

    b. Find the surface area and volume of the solid produced in part (a).

    c. Tape the straight side of a protractor, similar to the one at the right, to a pencil, as shown. Rotate the pencil. Is the solid produced by this rotating protractor different from the solid in part (a)? Explain. Draw a diagram to support your answer.

    b. Describe a method you might use to approximate the volume of the solid in part (c).

Communicate Your Answer

    3. How can you create a solid of revolution?

    4. Give some examples of real-life objects that are solids of revolution.

Name _____

1.4 Notetaking with Vocabulary

For use after Lesson 1.4

In your own words, write the meaning of each vocabulary term.

solid of revolution

axis of revolution

Notes:

1.4 Notetaking with Vocabulary (continued)

Extra Practice

In Exercises 1–4, sketch the solid produced by rotating the figure around the given axis.
Then identify and describe the solid.

1.

3.5
3.5
3.5
3.5

2.

7
7

3.

2 cm
8 cm
4 cm

4.

2 cm
8 cm
4 cm

In Exercises 5–8, sketch a two-dimensional shape and an axis of revolution that
forms the object shown.

5.

6.

1.4 **Notetaking with Vocabulary** (continued)

7.

8.

In Exercises 9 and 10, sketch and describe the solid produced by rotating the figure around the given axis. Then find its surface area and volume.

9.

10.

In Exercises 11 and 12, sketch and describe the solid that is produced when the region enclosed by the given equations is rotated around the given axis. Then find the volume of the solid.

11. $x = 0, y = 0, y = -x + 4$; y-axis

12. $x = 6, y = 0, y = 2x$; x-axis

Chapter 2 Maintaining Mathematical Proficiency

Evaluate.

1. $7 \cdot 3^2 + 11$

2. $10 - 3(3 + 1)^3$

3. $64 \div 4^2 + \dfrac{1}{2}$

4. $-99 \div 3^2 \cdot 5$

5. $\dfrac{1}{7}(7^2 + 28)$

6. $-\dfrac{1}{8}(8 + 24) - 2^2$

Graph the transformation of the figure.

7. Translate the rectangle 3 units left and 4 units up.

8. Reflect the right triangle in the *y*-axis. Then translate 3 units down.

9. Translate the trapezoid 2 units up. Then reflect in the *x*-axis.

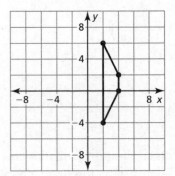

10. The point $(1, 1)$ is on $f(x)$. After a series of 3 transformations, $(1, 1)$ has been moved to $(2, -7)$. Write a function $g(x)$ that represents the transformations on $f(x)$.

2.1 Parent Functions and Transformations
For use with Exploration 2.1

Essential Question   What are the characteristics of some of the basic parent functions?

1   EXPLORATION: Identifying Basic Parent Functions

Work with a partner. Graphs of four basic parent functions are shown below.
Classify each function as *linear*, *absolute value*, *quadratic*, or *exponential*.
Justify your reasoning.

a.

b.

c.

d.
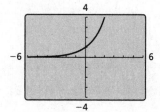

2.1 **Parent Functions and Transformations** (continued)

2 **EXPLORATION:** Identifying Basic Parent Functions

Work with a partner. Graphs of four basic parent functions that you will study later in this course are shown below. Classify each function as *square root*, *cube root*, *cubic*, or *reciprocal*. Justify your reasoning.

a.

b.

c.

d.

Communicate Your Answer

3. What are the characteristics of some of the basic parent functions?

4. Write an equation for each function whose graph is shown in Exploration 1. Then use a graphing calculator to verify that your equations are correct.

Name_____ Date_____

Notetaking with Vocabulary
For use after Lesson 2.1

In your own words, write the meaning of each vocabulary term.

parent function

transformation

translation

reflection

vertical stretch

vertical shrink

Core Concepts

Parent Functions

Family	Constant	Linear	Absolute Value	Quadratic
Rule	$f(x) = 1$	$f(x) = x$	$f(x) = |x|$	$f(x) = x^2$
Graph				
Domain	All real numbers	All real numbers	All real numbers	All real numbers
Range	$y = 1$	All real numbers	$y \geq 0$	$y \geq 0$

Notes:

2.1 **Notetaking with Vocabulary** (continued)

Extra Practice

In Exercises 1–4, identify the function family to which *f* belongs. Compare the graph of *f* to the graph of its parent function.

1.

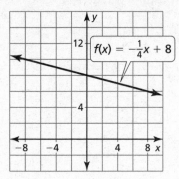

$f(x) = -\frac{1}{4}x + 8$

2.

$f(x) = -3$

3.

$f(x) = 5|x|$

4.

$f(x) = (x - 1)^2 + 4$

In Exercises 5–10, graph the function and its parent function. Then describe the transformation.

5. $f(x) = x - 7$

6. $f(x) = -9$

7. $f(x) = |x| + 1$

Name_____ Date_____

8. $h(x) = -x^2$

9. $f(x) = \frac{1}{8}x^2$

10. $g(x) = 6|x|$

11. Identify the function family of $f(x) = \frac{1}{3}|-x| + 4$ and describe the domain and range.

Use a graphing calculator to verify your answer.

12. The table shows the distance a biker rides in his first team relay competition.

Time (hours), x	1	2	3	4
Distance (miles), y	12	24	36	48

a. What type of function can you use to model the data? Explain.

b. If the biker's teammate rides at the same pace but leaves 1 hour later, what type of transformation does this represent?

Name _____ Date _____

Essential Question How do the graphs of $y = f(x) + k$, $y = f(x - h)$, and $y = -f(x)$ compare to the graph of the parent function f?

---

1 EXPLORATION: Transformations of the Parent Absolute Value Function

Go to *BigIdeasMath.com* for an interactive tool to investigate this exploration.

Work with a partner. Compare the graph of the function

$$y = |x| + k \qquad \text{Transformation}$$

to the graph of the parent function

$$f(x) = |x|. \qquad \text{Parent function}$$

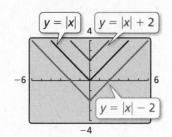

---

2 EXPLORATION: Transformations of the Parent Absolute Value Function

Go to *BigIdeasMath.com* for an interactive tool to investigate this exploration.

Work with a partner. Compare the graph of the function

$$y = |x - h| \qquad \text{Transformation}$$

to the graph of the parent function

$$f(x) = |x|. \qquad \text{Parent function}$$

2.2 **Transformations of Linear and Absolute Value Functions** (continued)

---

3 **EXPLORATION:** Transformation of the Parent Absolute Value Function

Go to *BigIdeasMath.com* for an interactive tool to investigate this exploration.

Work with a partner. Compare the graph of the function

$$y = -|x|$$ Transformation

to the graph of the parent function

$$f(x) = |x|.$$ Parent function

Communicate Your Answer

4. How do the graphs of $y = f(x) + k$, $y = f(x - h)$, and $y = -f(x)$ compare to the graph of the parent function f?

5. Compare the graph of each function to the graph of its parent function f. Use a graphing calculator to verify your answers are correct.

   a. $y = 2^x - 4$ **b.** $y = 2^{x+4}$ **c.** $y = -2^x$

   d. $y = x^2 + 1$ **e.** $y = (x - 1)^2$ **f.** $y = -x^2$

2.2 Notetaking with Vocabulary
For use after Lesson 2.2

Core Concepts

Horizontal Translations

The graph of $y = f(x - h)$ is a horizontal translation of the graph of $y = f(x)$, where $h \neq 0$.

Subtracting h from the **inputs** before evaluating the function shifts the graph left when $h < 0$ and right when $h > 0$.

Vertical Translations

The graph of $y = f(x) + k$ is a vertical translation of the graph of $y = f(x)$, where $k \neq 0$.

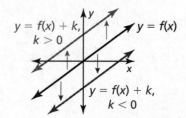

Adding k to the **outputs** shifts the graph down when $k < 0$ and up when $k > 0$.

Notes:

2.2   **Notetaking with Vocabulary** (continued)

Reflections in the *x*-axis

The graph of $y = -f(x)$ is a reflection in the *x*-axis of the graph of $y = f(x)$.

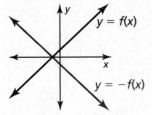

Multiplying the **outputs** by -1 changes their signs.

Notes:

Reflections in the *y*-axis

The graph of $y = f(-x)$ is a reflection in the *y*-axis of the graph of $y = f(x)$.

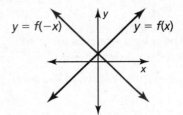

Multiplying the **inputs** by -1 changes their signs.

Horizontal Stretches and Shrinks

The graph of $y = f(ax)$ is a horizontal stretch or shrink by a factor of $\dfrac{1}{a}$ of the graph of $y = f(x)$, where $a > 0$ and $a \neq 1$.

Multiplying the **inputs** by a before evaluating the function stretches the graph horizontally (away from the *y*-axis) when $0 < a < 1$, and shrinks the graph horizontally (toward the *y*-axis) when $a > 1$.

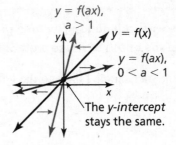

Notes:

Name _____ Date _____

Vertical Stretches and Shrinks

The graph of $y = a \bullet f(x)$ is a vertical stretch or shrink by a factor of a of the graph of $y = f(x)$, where $a > 0$ and $a \neq 1$.

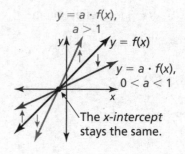

Multiplying the **outputs** by a stretches the graph vertically (away from the x-axis) when $a > 1$, and shrinks the graph vertically (toward the x-axis) when $0 < a < 1$.

Notes:

Extra Practice

In Exercises 1–9, write a function g whose graph represents the indicated transformation of the graph of f. Use a graphing calculator to check your answer.

1. $f(x) = \left| \frac{1}{3}x \right|$; translation 2 units to the left

2. $f(x) = -|x + 9| - 1$; translation 6 units down

3. $f(x) = -2x + 2$; translation 7 units down

2.2 **Notetaking with Vocabulary** (continued)

4. $f(x) = \frac{1}{2}x + 8$; reflection in the x-axis

5. $f(x) = 4 + |x + 1|$; reflection in the y-axis

6. $f(x) = -5x$; vertical shrink by a factor of $\frac{1}{5}$

7. $f(x) = |x + 3| + 2$; vertical stretch by a factor of 4

8. $f(x) = 3x - 9$; horizontal stretch by a factor of 6

9. $f(x) = -|8x| - 4$; horizontal shrink by a factor of $\frac{1}{4}$

10. Consider the function $f(x) = |x|$. Write a function g whose graph represents a reflection in the x-axis followed by a horizontal stretch by a factor of 3 and a translation 5 units down of the graph of f.

11. Which of the transformation(s) in Section 2.2 will *not* change the y-intercept of $f(x) = |x| + 3$?

Name_____ Date _____

2.3 Modeling with Linear Functions
For use with Exploration 2.3

Essential Question How can you use a linear function to model and analyze a real-life situation?

1 EXPLORATION: Modeling with a Linear Function

Go to *BigIdeasMath.com* for an interactive tool to investigate this exploration.

Work with a partner. A company purchases a copier for $12,000. The spreadsheet shows how the copier depreciates over an 8-year period.

	A	B
1	Year, *t*	Value, *V*
2	0	$12,000
3	1	$10,750
4	2	$9,500
5	3	$8,250
6	4	$7,000
7	5	$5,750
8	6	$4,500
9	7	$3,250
10	8	$2,000

a. Write a linear function to represent the value *V* of the copier as a function of the number *t* of years.

b. Sketch a graph of the function. Explain why this type of depreciation is called *straight line depreciation*.

c. Interpret the slope of the graph in the context of the problem.

2.3 **Modeling with Linear Functions** (continued)

2 **EXPLORATION:** Modeling with Linear Functions

Work with a partner. Match each description of the situation with its corresponding graph. Explain your reasoning.

a. A person gives $20 per week to a friend to repay a $200 loan.

b. An employee receives $12.50 per hour plus $2 for each unit produced per hour.

c. A sales representative receives $30 per day for food plus $0.565 for each mile driven.

d. A computer that was purchased for $750 depreciates $100 per year.

A.   **B.**   **C.**   **D.**

Communicate Your Answer

3. How can you use a linear function to model and analyze a real-life situation?

4. Use the Internet or some other reference to find a real-life example of straight line depreciation.

a. Use a spreadsheet to show the depreciation.

b. Write a function that models the depreciation.

c. Sketch a graph of the function.

2.3 Notetaking with Vocabulary
For use after Lesson 2.3

In your own words, write the meaning of each vocabulary term.

line of fit

line of best fit

correlation coefficient

Core Concepts

Writing an Equation of a Line

Given slope *m* and *y*-intercept *b*   Use slope-intercept form:

$$y = mx + b$$

Given slope *m* and a point (x_1, y_1)   Use point-slope form:

$$y - y_1 = m(x - x_1)$$

Given points (x_1, y_1) and (x_2, y_2)   First use the slope formula to find *m*.
Then use point-slope form with either given point.

Notes:

Name_____ Date_____

Finding a Line of Fit

Step 1 Create a scatter plot of the data.

Step 2 Sketch the line that most closely appears to follow the trend given by the data points. There should be about as many points above the line as below it.

Step 3 Choose two points on the line and estimate the coordinates of each point. These points do not have to be original data points.

Step 4 Write an equation of the line that passes through the two points from Step 3. This equation is a model for the data.

Notes:

Extra Practice

In Exercises 1–3, use the graph to write an equation of the line and interpret the slope.

1.

2.

3.

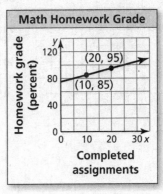

2.3 **Notetaking with Vocabulary** (continued)

4. The cost of parking in a parking garage in Chicago is represented by the equation $y = 15x + 20$ where y is the total cost (in dollars) and x is the time (in hours). The table shows the total cost to park in a parking garage in Denver. Which city's parking garage charges more per hour and by how much more? After how many hours would parking in both cities cost the same?

Hours, x	2	3	4	5
Cost, y	43	51	59	67

In Exercises 5–7, use the *linear regression* feature on a graphing calculator to find an equation of the line of best fit for the data. Find and interpret the correlation coefficient.

5.

6.

7.

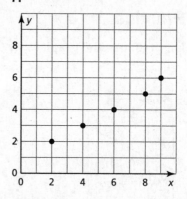

2.4 Solving Linear Systems
For use with Exploration 2.4

Essential Question How can you determine the number of solutions of a linear system?

A linear system is *consistent* when it has at least one solution. A linear system is *inconsistent* when it has no solution.

1 EXPLORATION: Recognizing Graphs of Linear Systems

Work with a partner. Match each linear system with its corresponding graph. Explain your reasoning. Then classify the system as *consistent* or *inconsistent*.

a. $2x - 3y = 3$
  $-4x + 6y = 6$

b. $2x - 3y = 3$
  $x + 2y = 5$

c. $2x - 3y = 3$
  $-4x + 6y = -6$

A.

B.

C.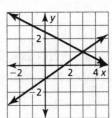

2 EXPLORATION: Solving Systems of Linear Equations

Work with a partner. Solve each linear system by substitution or elimination. Then use the graph of the system on the next page to check your solution.

a. $2x + y = 5$
  $x - y = 1$

b. $x + 3y = 1$
  $-x + 2y = 4$

c. $x + y = 0$
  $3x + 2y = 1$

2.4 **Solving Linear Systems** (continued)

2 **EXPLORATION:** Solving Systems of Linear Equations (continued)

a.   b.   c.

Communicate Your Answer

3. How can you determine the number of solutions of a linear system?

4. Suppose you were given a system of *three* linear equations in *three* variables. Explain how you would approach solving such a system.

5. Apply your strategy in Question 4 to solve the linear system.

$$x + y + z = 1 \quad \text{Equation 1}$$
$$x - y - z = 3 \quad \text{Equation 2}$$
$$-x - y + z = -1 \quad \text{Equation 3}$$

2.4 Notetaking with Vocabulary
For use after Lesson 2.4

In your own words, write the meaning of each vocabulary term.

linear equation in three variables

system of three linear equations

solution of a system of three linear equations

ordered triple

Core Concepts

Solving a Three-Variable System

Step 1 Rewrite the linear system in three variables as a linear system in two variables by using the substitution or elimination method.

Step 2 Solve the new linear system for both of its variables.

Step 3 Substitute the values found in Step 2 into one of the original equations and solve for the remaining variable.

When you obtain a false equation, such as $0 = 1$, in any of the steps, the system has no solution.

When you do not obtain a false equation, but obtain an identity such as $0 = 0$, the system has infinitely many solutions.

Notes:

2.4 **Notetaking with Vocabulary** (continued)

Extra Practice

In Exercises 1–3, solve the system using the elimination method.

1. $x + 2y - 3z = 11$
$2x + y - 2z = 9$
$4x + 3y + z = 16$

2. $x - y + 3z = 19$
$-2x + 2y - 6z = 9$
$3x + 5y + 2z = 3$

3. $x + y - z = -9$
$2x - 3y + 2z = 13$
$3x - 5y - 6z = -15$

In Exercises 4–6, solve the system using the substitution method.

4. $x + y + z = 4$
$x + y - z = 4$
$3x + 3y + z = 12$

5. $2x + 3y - z = 9$
$x - 3y + z = -6$
$3x + y - 4z = 31$

6. $x + 2y - 5z = -12$
$2x + 2y - 3z = -2$
$3x - 4y - z = 11$

7. You found $6.60 on the ground at school, all in nickels, dimes, and quarters. You have twice as many quarters as dimes and 42 coins in all. How many of each type of coin do you have?

2.4   **Notetaking with Vocabulary** (continued)

8. Find the values of a, b, and c so that the linear system below has $(3, -2, 1)$ as its only solution. Explain your reasoning.

$$3x + 2y - 7z = a$$
$$x + 3y + z = b$$
$$4x - 2y - z = c$$

9. Does the system of linear equations have more than one solution? Justify your answer.

$$\frac{1}{2}x - \frac{3}{8}y + \frac{1}{8}z = -\frac{5}{4}$$
$$\frac{1}{2}x + \frac{1}{4}y + \frac{3}{4}z = 0$$
$$-x + 2y - 5z = 17$$

10. If $\angle A$ is three times as large as $\angle B$, and $\angle B$ is 30° smaller than $\angle C$, what are the measures of angles A, B, and C?

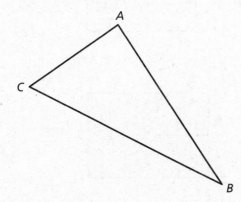

2.5 Transformations of Quadratic Functions
For use with Exploration 2.5

Essential Question How do the constants *a*, *h*, and *k* affect the graph of the quadratic function $g(x) = a(x-h)^2 + k$?

 1 EXPLORATION: Identifying Graphs of Quadratic Functions

Go to *BigIdeasMath.com* for an interactive tool to investigate this exploration.

Work with a partner. Match each quadratic function with its graph. Explain your reasoning. Then use a graphing calculator to verify that your answer is correct.

a. $g(x) = -(x-2)^2$ **b.** $g(x) = (x-2)^2 + 2$ **c.** $g(x) = -(x+2)^2 - 2$

d. $g(x) = 0.5(x-2)^2 - 2$ **e.** $g(x) = 2(x-2)^2$ **f.** $g(x) = -(x+2)^2 + 2$

A.

B.

C.

D.

E.

F.

2.5 Transformations of Quadratic Functions (continued)

Communicate Your Answer

2. How do the constants a, h, and k affect the graph of the quadratic function
$g(x) = a(x - h)^2 + k$?

3. Write the equation of the quadratic function whose graph is shown. Explain your
reasoning. Then use a graphing calculator to verify that your equation is correct.

2.5 Notetaking with Vocabulary
For use after Lesson 2.5

In your own words, write the meaning of each vocabulary term.

quadratic function

parabola

vertex of a parabola

vertex form

Core Concepts

Horizontal Translations

$$f(x) = x^2$$

$$f(x - h) = (x - h)^2$$

- shifts left when $h < 0$

- shifts right when $h > 0$

Vertical Translations

$$f(x) = x^2$$

$$f(x) + k = x^2 + k$$

- shifts down when $k < 0$

- shifts up when $k > 0$

Notes:

2.5 Notetaking with Vocabulary (continued)

Reflections in the *x*-Axis

$$f(x) = x^2$$
$$-f(x) = -(x^2) = -x^2$$

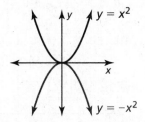

flips over the *x*-axis

Reflections in the *y*-Axis

$$f(x) = x^2$$
$$f(-x) = (-x)^2 = x^2$$

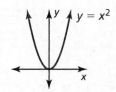

$y = x^2$ is its own

reflection in the *y*-axis.

Horizontal Stretches and Shrinks

$$f(x) = x^2$$
$$f(ax) = (ax)^2$$

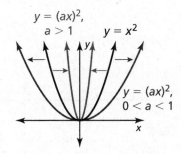

- horizontal stretch (away from *y*-axis) when $0 < a < 1$

- horizontal shrink (toward *y*-axis) when $a > 1$

Vertical Stretches and Shrinks

$$f(x) = x^2$$
$$a \bullet f(x) = ax^2$$

- vertical stretch (away from *x*-axis) when $a > 1$

- vertical shrink (toward *x*-axis) when $0 < a < 1$

Notes:

2.5 Notetaking with Vocabulary (continued)

Extra Practice

In Exercises 1–6, describe the transformation of $f(x) = x^2$ represented by g.
Then graph the function.

1. $g(x) = x^2 + 4$

2. $g(x) = (x - 1)^2 - 3$

3. $g(x) = -(x + 9)^2$

4. $g(x) = x^2 - 7$

5. $g(x) = \frac{1}{3}x^2 - 6$

6. $g(x) = (-4x)^2$

7. Consider the function $f(x) = -10(x - 5)^2 + 7$. Describe the transformation of the graph of the parent quadratic function. Then identify the vertex.

Name_____ Date _____

2.6 Characteristics of Quadratic Functions
For use with Exploration 2.6

Essential Question What type of symmetry does the graph of $f(x) = a(x - h)^2 + k$ have and how can you describe this symmetry?

1 EXPLORATION: Parabolas and Symmetry

Work with a partner.

a. Complete the table. Then use the values in the table to sketch the graph of the function $f(x) = \frac{1}{2}x^2 - 2x - 2$ on graph paper.

x	−2	−1	0	1	2
f(x)					

x	3	4	5	6
f(x)				

b. Use the results in part (a) to identify the vertex of the parabola.

c. Find a vertical line on your graph paper so that when you fold the paper, the left portion of the graph coincides with the right portion of the graph. What is the equation of this line? How does it relate to the vertex?

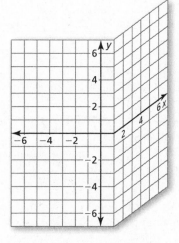

d. Show that the vertex form $f(x) = \frac{1}{2}(x - 2)^2 - 4$ is equivalent to the function given in part (a).

2.6 **Characteristics of Quadratic Functions** (continued)

2 **EXPLORATION:** Parabolas and Symmetry

Work with a partner. Repeat Exploration 1 for the function given by $f(x) = -\frac{1}{3}x^2 + 2x + 3 = -\frac{1}{3}(x - 3)^2 + 6$.

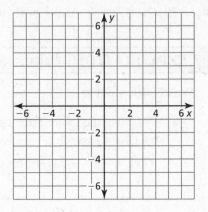

x	−2	−1	0	1	2
f(x)					

x	3	4	5	6
f(x)				

Communicate Your Answer

3. What type of symmetry does the graph of $f(x) = a(x - h)^2 + k$ have and how can you describe this symmetry?

4. Describe the symmetry of each graph. Then use a graphing calculator to verify your answer.

   a. $f(x) = -(x - 1)^2 + 4$ b. $f(x) = (x + 1)^2 - 2$ c. $f(x) = 2(x - 3)^2 + 1$

   d. $f(x) = \frac{1}{2}(x + 2)^2$ e. $f(x) = -2x^2 + 3$ f. $f(x) = 3(x - 5)^2 + 2$

Name_____ Date_____

2.6 Notetaking with Vocabulary
For use after Lesson 2.6

In your own words, write the meaning of each vocabulary term.

axis of symmetry

standard form

minimum value

maximum value

intercept form

Core Concepts

Properties of the Graph of $f(x) = ax^2 + bx + c$

$y = ax^2 + bx + c, a > 0$ $y = ax^2 + bx + c, a < 0$

- The parabola opens up when $a > 0$ and open down when $a < 0$.

- The graph is narrower than the graph of $f(x) = x^2$ when $|a| > 1$ and wider when $|a| < 1$.

- The axis of symmetry is $x = -\dfrac{b}{2a}$ and the vertex is $\left(-\dfrac{b}{2a}, f\left(-\dfrac{b}{2a}\right)\right)$.

- The y-intercept is c. So, the point $(0, c)$ is on the parabola.

Notes:

2.6 **Notetaking with Vocabulary** (continued)

Minimum and Maximum Values

For the quadratic function $f(x) = ax^2 + bx + c$, the y-coordinate of the vertex is the **minimum value** of the function when $a > 0$ and the **maximum value** when $a < 0$.

$a > 0$

$a < 0$

- Minimum value: $f\left(-\dfrac{b}{2a}\right)$

- Domain: All real numbers

- Range: $y \geq f\left(-\dfrac{b}{2a}\right)$

- Decreasing to the left of $x = -\dfrac{b}{2a}$

- Increasing to the right of $x = -\dfrac{b}{2a}$

- Maximum value: $f\left(-\dfrac{b}{2a}\right)$

- Domain: All real numbers

- Range: $y \leq f\left(-\dfrac{b}{2a}\right)$

- Increasing to the left of $x = -\dfrac{b}{2a}$

- Decreasing to the right of $x = -\dfrac{b}{2a}$

Notes:

Properties of the Graph of $f(x) = a(x - p)(x - q)$

- Because $f(p) = 0$ and $f(q) = 0$, p and q are the x-intercepts of the graph of the function.

- The axis of symmetry is halfway between $(p, 0)$ and $(q, 0)$.

  So, the axis of symmetry is $x = \dfrac{p + q}{2}$.

- The parabola opens up when $a > 0$ and opens down when $a < 0$.

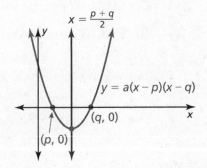

Notes:

2.6 **Notetaking with Vocabulary** (continued)

Extra Practice

In Exercises 1–3, graph the function. Label the vertex and axis of symmetry. Find the minimum or maximum value of the function. Describe the domain and range of the function, and where the function is increasing and decreasing.

1. $f(x) = (x + 1)^2$ **2.** $y = -2(x - 4)^2 - 5$ **3.** $t(x) = \frac{3}{2}x^2 - 3x - 1$

In Exercises 4 and 5, graph the function. Label the *x*-intercept(s), vertex, and axis of symmetry.

4. $f(x) = 4(x + 4)(x - 3)$ **5.** $f(x) = -7x(x - 6)$

 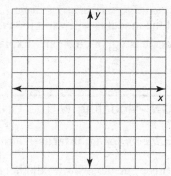

6. A softball player hits a ball whose path is modeled by $f(x) = -0.0005x^2 + 0.2127x + 3$, where *x* is the distance from home plate (in feet) and *y* is the height of the ball above the ground (in feet). What is the highest point this ball will reach? If the ball was hit to center field which has an 8 foot fence located 410 feet from home plate, was this hit a home run? Explain.

2.7 Modeling with Quadratic Functions
For use with Exploration 2.7

Essential Question How can you use a quadratic function to model a real-life situation?

1 EXPLORATION: Modeling with a Quadratic Function

Work with a partner. The graph shows a quadratic function of the form $P(t) = at^2 + bt + c$ which approximates the yearly profits for a company, where $P(t)$ is the profit in year t.

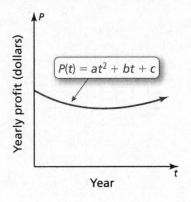

a. Is the value of a positive, negative, or zero? Explain.

b. Write an expression in terms of a and b that represents the year t when the company made the least profit.

c. The company made the same yearly profits in 2004 and 2012. Estimate the year in which the company made the least profit.

d. Assume that the model is still valid today. Are the yearly profits currently increasing, decreasing, or constant? Explain.

2 EXPLORATION: Modeling with a Graphing Calculator

Go to *BigIdeasMath.com* for an interactive tool to investigate this exploration.

Work with a partner. The table shows the heights h (in feet) of a wrench t seconds after it has been dropped from a building under construction.

Time, t	0	1	2	3	4
Height, h	400	384	336	256	144

a. Use a graphing calculator to create a scatter plot of the data, as shown at the right. Explain why the data appear to fit a quadratic model.

2.7 **Modeling with Quadratic Functions** (continued)

2 **EXPLORATION:** Modeling with a Graphing Calculator (continued)

   b. Use the *quadratic regression* feature to find a quadratic model for the data.

   c. Graph the quadratic function on the same screen as the scatter plot to verify that it fits the data.

   d. When does the wrench hit the ground? Explain.

Communicate Your Answer

   3. How can you use a quadratic function to model a real-life situation?

   4. Use the Internet or some other reference to find examples of real-life situations that can be modeled by quadratic functions.

2.7 Notetaking with Vocabulary
For use after Lesson 2.7

In your own words, write the meaning of each vocabulary term.

average rate of change

first differences

second differences

system of three linear equations

Quadratic Formula

Core Concepts

Writing Quadratic Equations

Given a point and the vertex (h, k)	Use vertex form: $y = a(x - h)^2 + k$
Given a point and x-intercepts p and q	Use intercept form: $y = a(x - p)(x - q)$
Given three points	Write and solve a system of three equations in three variables.

Notes:

2.7 **Notetaking with Vocabulary** (continued)

Extra Practice

In Exercises 1–4, write an equation of the parabola in vertex form.

1.

2.

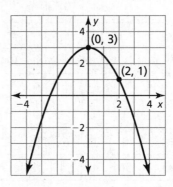

3. passes through $(-3, 0)$ and has vertex $(-1, -8)$

4. passes through $(-4, 7)$ and has vertex $(-2, 5)$

In Exercises 5–8, write an equation of the parabola in intercept form.

5.

6.

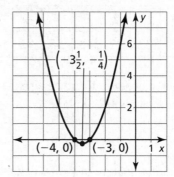

7. x-intercepts of -5 and 8; passes through $(1, 84)$

8. x-intercepts of 7 and 10; passes through $(-2, 27)$

2.7 Notetaking with Vocabulary (continued)

In Exercises 9–11, analyze the differences in the outputs to determine whether the data are *linear*, *quadratic* or *neither*. If linear or quadratic, write an equation that fits the data.

9.

Time (seconds), *x*	1	2	3	4	5	6
Distance (feet), *y*	424	416	376	304	200	64

10.

Time (days), *x*	0	3	6	9	12	15
Height (inches), *y*	36	30	24	18	12	6

11.

Time (years), *x*	1	2	3	4	5	6
Profit (dollars), *y*	5	15	45	135	405	1215

12. The table shows a university's budget (in millions of dollars) over a 10-year period, where $x = 0$ represents the first year in the 10-year period.

Years, *x*	0	1	2	3	4	5	6	7	8	9
Budget, *y*	65	32	22	40	65	92	114	128	140	150

   a. Use a graphing calculator to create a scatter plot. Which better represents the data, a line or a parabola? Explain.

   b. Use the *regression* feature of your calculator to find the model that best fits the data.

   c. Use the model in part (b) to predict when the budget of the university is $500,000,000.00.

Chapter 3 **Maintaining Mathematical Proficiency**

Simplify the expression.

1. $-8x - 9x$

2. $25r - 5 + 7r - r$

3. $5 + 13t - 9 + t - 8t$

4. $4 - (a + 2)$

5. $3 + 6(3x - 5) + x$

6. $3y - (2y - 5) + 11$

7. $-3(h + 7) - 7(10 - h)$

8. $5 - 8x^2 + 5x + 8x^2$

9. $6(x^2 - 2) + x(3 - x)$

Solve the equation by factoring.

10. $x^2 + 8x + 15 = 0$

11. $x^2 + 3x - 18 = 0$

12. $x^2 - 2x - 8 = 0$

13. $x^2 + 12x = -36$

14. $2x^2 - 24 = 8x$

15. $3x^2 = 18x - 24$

16. $5x^2 + 2 = -7x$

17. $2x = 15 - 8x^2$

18. $17x - 7 = 6x^2$

Name _____ Date _____

Essential Question What are some common characteristics of the graphs of cubic and quartic polynomial functions?

1 **EXPLORATION:** Identifying Graphs of Polynomial Functions

Go to *BigIdeasMath.com* for an interactive tool to investigate this exploration.

Work with a partner. Match each polynomial function with its graph. Explain your reasoning. Use a graphing calculator to verify your answers.

a. $f(x) = x^3 - x$ 　　　　**b.** $f(x) = -x^3 + x$ 　　　　**c.** $f(x) = -x^4 + 1$

d. $f(x) = x^4$ 　　　　**e.** $f(x) = x^3$ 　　　　**f.** $f(x) = x^4 - x^2$

A.

B.

C.

D.

E.

F.

3.1 **Graphing Polynomial Functions** (continued)

---

2 **EXPLORATION:** Identifying *x*-Intercepts of Polynomial Graphs

Work with a partner. Each of the polynomial graphs in Exploration 1 has *x*-intercept(s) of −1 , 0, or 1. Identify the *x*-intercept(s) of each graph. Explain how you can verify your answers.

Communicate Your Answer

3. What are some common characteristics of the graphs of cubic and quartic polynomial functions?

4. Determine whether each statement is *true* or *false*. Justify your answer.

   a. When the graph of a cubic polynomial function rises to the left, it falls to the right.

   b. When the graph of a quartic polynomial function falls to the left, it rises to the right.

3.1 Notetaking with Vocabulary
For use after Lesson 3.1

In your own words, write the meaning of each vocabulary term.

polynomial

polynomial function

end behavior

Core Concepts

End Behavior of Polynomial Functions

Degree: odd

Leading coefficient: positive

$f(x) \to +\infty$ as $x \to +\infty$
$f(x) \to -\infty$ as $x \to -\infty$

Degree: odd

Leading coefficient: negative

$f(x) \to +\infty$ as $x \to -\infty$
$f(x) \to -\infty$ as $x \to +\infty$

Degree: even

Leading coefficient: positive

$f(x) \to +\infty$ as $x \to -\infty$
$f(x) \to +\infty$ as $x \to +\infty$

Degree: even

Leading coefficient: negative

$f(x) \to -\infty$ as $x \to -\infty$
$f(x) \to -\infty$ as $x \to +\infty$

Notes:

Name_____ Date_____

Extra Practice

In Exercises 1–4, decide whether the function is a polynomial function. If so, write it in standard form and state its degree, type, and leading coefficient.

1. $f(x) = 2x^2 - 3x^4 + 6x + 1$

2. $m(x) = -\frac{3}{7}x^3 + \frac{7}{x} - 3$

3. $g(x) = \sqrt{15}x + \sqrt{5}$

4. $p(x) = -2\sqrt{3} + 3x - 2x^2$

In Exercises 5 and 6, evaluate the function for the given value of x.

5. $h(x) = -x^3 - 2x^2 - 3x + 4;\ x = 2$

6. $g(x) = x^4 - 32x^2 + 256;\ x = -4$

In Exercises 7 and 8, describe the end behavior of the graph of the function.

7. $f(x) = -3x^6 + 4x^2 - 3x + 6$

8. $f(x) = \frac{4}{5}x + 6x + 3x^5 - 3x^3 - 2$

9. Describe the degree and leading coefficient of the polynomial function using the graph.

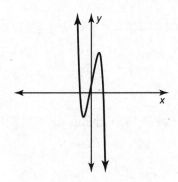

3.1 **Notetaking with Vocabulary** (continued)

In Exercises 10 and 11, graph the polynomial function.

10. $p(x) = 16 - x^4$

11. $g(x) = x^2 + 3x^5 - x$

12. Sketch a graph of the polynomial function f if

f is increasing when $x < -1$ and $0 < x < 1$,

f is decreasing when $-1 < x < 0$ and $x > 1$,

and $f(x) < 0$ for all real numbers.

Describe the degree and leading coefficient of the function f.

13. The number of students S (in thousands) who graduate in four years from a university can be modeled by the function $S(t) = -\frac{1}{4}t^3 + t^2 + 23$, where t is the number of years since 2010.

a. Use a graphing calculator to graph the function for the interval $0 \le t \le 5$. Describe the behavior of the graph on this interval.

b. What is the average rate of change in the number of four-year graduates from 2010 to 2015?

c. Do you think this model can be used for years before 2010 or after 2015? Explain your reasoning.

3.2 Adding, Subtracting, and Multiplying Polynomials
For use with Exploration 3.2

Essential Question How can you cube a binomial?

1 EXPLORATION: Cubing Binomials

Work with a partner. Find each product. Show your steps.

a. $(x + 1)^3 = (x + 1)(x + 1)^2$ Rewrite as a product of first and second powers.

$= (x + 1)$ _____   Multiply second power.

$=$ _____   Multiply binomial and trinomial.

$=$ _____   Write in standard form, $ax^3 + bx^2 + cx + d$.

b. $(a + b)^3 = (a + b)(a + b)^2$ Rewrite as a product of first and second powers.

$= (a + b)$ _____   Multiply second power.

$=$ _____   Multiply binomial and trinomial.

$=$ _____   Write in standard form.

c. $(x - 1)^3 = (x - 1)(x - 1)^2$ Rewrite as a product of first and second powers.

$= (x - 1)$ _____   Multiply second power.

$=$ _____   Multiply binomial and trinomial.

$=$ _____   Write in standard form.

d. $(a - b)^3 = (a - b)(a - b)^2$ Rewrite as a product of first and second powers.

$= (a - b)$ _____   Multiply second power.

$=$ _____   Multiply binomial and trinomial.

$=$ _____   Write in standard form.

3.2 **Adding, Subtracting, and Multiplying Polynomials** (continued)

---

2 EXPLORATION: Generalizing Patterns for Cubing a Binomial

Work with a partner.

a. Use the results of Exploration 1 to describe a pattern for the coefficients of the terms when you expand the cube of a binomial. How is your pattern related to Pascal's Triangle, shown at the right?

b. Use the results of Exploration 1 to describe a pattern for the exponents of the terms in the expansion of a cube of a binomial.

c. Explain how you can use the patterns you described in parts (a) and (b) to find the product $(2x - 3)^3$. Then find this product.

Communicate Your Answer

3. How can you cube a binomial?

4. Find each product.

a. $(x + 2)^3$

b. $(x - 2)^3$

c. $(2x - 3)^3$

d. $(x - 3)^3$

e. $(-2x + 3)^3$

f. $(3x - 5)^3$

3.2 Notetaking with Vocabulary
For use after Lesson 3.2

In your own words, write the meaning of each vocabulary term.

Pascal's Triangle

Binomial Theorem

Core Concepts

Special Product Patterns

Sum and Difference	Example
$(a + b)(a - b) = a^2 - b^2$	$(x + 3)(x - 3) = x^2 - 9$

Square of a Binomial	Example
$(a + b)^2 = a^2 + 2ab + b^2$	$(y + 4)^2 = y^2 + 8y + 16$
$(a - b)^2 = a^2 - 2ab + b^2$	$(2t - 5)^2 = 4t^2 - 20t + 25$

Cube of a Binomial	Example
$(a + b)^3 = a^3 + 3a^2b + 3ab^2 + b^3$	$(z + 3)^3 = z^3 + 9z^2 + 27z + 27$
$(a - b)^3 = a^3 - 3a^2b + 3ab^2 - b^3$	$(m - 2)^3 = m^3 - 6m^2 + 12m - 8$

Notes:

3.2 **Notetaking with Vocabulary** (continued)

Pascal's Triangle

In Pascal's Triangle, the first and last numbers in each row are 1. Every number other than 1 is the sum of the closest two numbers in the row directly above it. The numbers in Pascal's Triangle are the same numbers that are the coefficients of binomial expansions, as shown in the first six rows.

	n	$(a+b)^n$	Binomial Expansion	Pascal's Triangle
0th row	0	$(a+b)^0 =$	1	1
1st row	1	$(a+b)^1 =$	$1a + 1b$	1 1
2nd row	2	$(a+b)^2 =$	$1a^2 + 2ab + 1b^2$	1 2 1
3rd row	3	$(a+b)^3 =$	$1a^3 + 3a^2b + 3ab^2 + 1b^3$	1 3 3 1
4th row	4	$(a+b)^4 =$	$1a^4 + 4a^3b + 6a^2b^2 + 4ab^3 + 1b^4$	1 4 6 4 1
5th row	5	$(a+b)^5 =$	$1a^5 + 5a^4b + 10a^3b^2 + 10a^2b^3 + 5ab^4 + 1b^5$	1 5 10 10 5 1

Notes:

The Binomial Theorem

For any positive integer n, the binomial expansion of $(a+b)^n$ is

$$(a+b)^n = {}_nC_0 a^n b^0 + {}_nC_1 a^{n-1}b^1 + {}_nC_2 a^{n-2}b^2 + \cdots + {}_nC_n a^0 b^n.$$

Notice that each term in the expansion of $(a+b)^n$ has the form ${}_nC_r a^{n-r}b^r$, where r is an integer from 0 to n.

Notes:

Name_____ Date_____

Extra Practice

In Exercises 1–3, find the sum or difference.

1. $\left(-4x^2 - 6x + 18\right) + \left(-x^2 + 7x + 8\right)$

2. $\left(6x^2 - 12x + 48\right) - \left(-x^2 + 24x - 63\right)$

3. $\left(-11x^4 - x^3 - 3x^2 + 10x - 2\right) - \left(-11x^4 + 5x^2 - 7x + 13\right)$

In Exercises 4–9, find the product.

4. $\left(x^4 - 10x^2 + 25\right)\left(3x^2 - 6x - 1\right)$

5. $(2x - 3)(6 - x)(4 - 5x)$

6. $(3y - 8)(3y + 8)$

7. $(2v - 1)^3$

In Exercises 8 and 9, use Pascal's Triangle to expand the binomial.

8. $(4t - 2)^4$

9. $(g + 6)^5$

10. Use the Binomial Theorem to write the binomial expansion of $\left(2x^4 + y^3\right)^3$.

3.3 Dividing Polynomials
For use with Exploration 3.3

Essential Question How can you use the factors of a cubic polynomial to solve a division problem involving the polynomial?

---

1 EXPLORATION: Dividing Polynomials

Go to *BigIdeasMath.com* for an interactive tool to investigate this exploration.

Work with a partner. Match each division statement with the graph of the related cubic polynomial $f(x)$. Explain your reasoning. Use a graphing calculator to verify your answers.

a. $\dfrac{f(x)}{x} = (x - 1)(x + 2)$ **b.** $\dfrac{f(x)}{x - 1} = (x - 1)(x + 2)$

c. $\dfrac{f(x)}{x + 1} = (x - 1)(x + 2)$ **d.** $\dfrac{f(x)}{x - 2} = (x - 1)(x + 2)$

e. $\dfrac{f(x)}{x + 2} = (x - 1)(x + 2)$ **f.** $\dfrac{f(x)}{x - 3} = (x - 1)(x + 2)$

A.

B.

C.

D.

E.

F.

3.3 **Dividing Polynomials** (continued)

---

2 **EXPLORATION:** Dividing Polynomials

Work with a partner. Use the results of Exploration 1 to find each quotient. Write your answers in standard form. Check your answers by multiplying.

a. $\left(x^3 + x^2 - 2x\right) \div x$

b. $\left(x^3 - 3x + 2\right) \div (x - 1)$

c. $\left(x^3 + 2x^2 - x - 2\right) \div (x + 1)$

d. $\left(x^3 - x^2 - 4x + 4\right) \div (x - 2)$

e. $\left(x^3 + 3x^2 - 4\right) \div (x + 2)$

f. $\left(x^3 - 2x^2 - 5x + 6\right) \div (x - 3)$

Communicate Your Answer

3. How can you use the factors of a cubic polynomial to solve a division problem involving the polynomial?

3.3 Notetaking with Vocabulary
For use after Lesson 3.3

In your own words, write the meaning of each vocabulary term.

polynomial long division

synthetic division

Core Concepts

The Remainder Theorem

If a polynomial $f(x)$ is divided by $x - k$, then the remainder is $r = f(k)$.

Notes:

Name_____ Date_____

Extra Practice

In Exercises 1–4, divide using polynomial long division.

1. $\left(x^2 + 6x + 12\right) \div (x - 3)$

2. $\left(x^3 - 4x^2\right) \div \left(x^2 - 16\right)$

3. $\left(4x^3 + 13x^2 + 27x + 6\right) \div (4x + 1)$

4. $\left(x^4 + 2x^3 + 5x^2 + 3x\right) \div \left(x^2 - x\right)$

In Exercises 5–8, divide using synthetic division.

5. $\left(x^2 - 10x + 2\right) \div (x - 2)$

6. $\left(x^3 + 4x^2 + 6x + 4\right) \div (x + 2)$

7. $\left(2x^3 - 54\right) \div (x + 3)$

8. $\left(2x^4 - 11x^3 + 11x^2 + 4x + 4\right) \div (x - 4)$

3.3 **Notetaking with Vocabulary** (continued)

In Exercises 9–12, match the equivalent expressions. Justify your answers.

9. $\left(x^2 - x - 8\right) \div \left(x - 4\right)$

    A. $x + 3 + \dfrac{4}{x - 4}$

10. $\left(x^2 - x + 8\right) \div \left(x - 4\right)$

    B. $x + 5 + \dfrac{12}{x - 4}$

11. $\left(x^2 + x - 8\right) \div \left(x - 4\right)$

    C. $x + 5 + \dfrac{28}{x - 4}$

12. $\left(x^2 + x + 8\right) \div \left(x - 4\right)$

    D. $x + 3 + \dfrac{20}{x - 4}$

In Exercises 13–16, use synthetic division to evaluate the function for the indicated value of x.

13. $f(x) = -3x^3 + 4x^2 - 17x - 6; x = 2$

14. $f(x) = -x^4 + x^2 + 4; x = -1$

15. $f(x) = x^3 - 10x^2 + 31x - 30; x = -5$

16. $f(x) = x^3 + 8x + 27; x = 3$

17. What is the value of k such that $\left(-x^4 + 5x^2 + kx - 8\right) \div \left(x - 4\right)$ has a remainder of 0?

3.4 Factoring Polynomials
For use with Exploration 3.4

Essential Question How can you factor a polynomial?

1 EXPLORATION: Factoring Polynomials

Work with a partner. Match each polynomial equation with the graph of its related polynomial function. Use the *x*-intercepts of the graph to write each polynomial in factored form. Explain your reasoning.

a. $x^2 + 5x + 4 = 0$

b. $x^3 - 2x^2 - x + 2 = 0$

c. $x^3 + x^2 - 2x = 0$

d. $x^3 - x = 0$

e. $x^4 - 5x^2 + 4 = 0$

f. $x^4 - 2x^3 - x^2 + 2x = 0$

A.

B.

C.

D.

E.

F.

3.4 **Factoring Polynomials** (continued)

2 **EXPLORATION:** Factoring Polynomials

Work with a partner. Use the *x*-intercepts of the graph of the polynomial function to write each polynomial in factored form. Explain your reasoning. Check your answers by multiplying.

a. $f(x) = x^2 - x - 2$

b. $f(x) = x^3 - x^2 - 2x$

c. $f(x) = x^3 - 2x^2 - 3x$

d. $f(x) = x^3 - 3x^2 - x + 3$

e. $f(x) = x^4 + 2x^3 - x^2 - 2x$

f. $f(x) = x^4 - 10x^2 + 9$

Communicate Your Answer

3. How can you factor a polynomial?

4. What information can you obtain about the graph of a polynomial function written in factored form?

3.4 Notetaking with Vocabulary
For use after Lesson 3.4

In your own words, write the meaning of each vocabulary term.

factored completely

factor by grouping

quadratic form

Core Concepts

Special Factoring Patterns

Sum of Two Cubes

$a^3 + b^3 = (a + b)(a^2 - ab + b^2)$

Example

$64x^3 + 1 = (4x)^3 + 1^3$
$= (4x + 1)(16x^2 - 4x + 1)$

Difference of Two Cubes

$a^3 - b^3 = (a - b)(a^2 + ab + b^2)$

Example

$27x^3 - 8 = (3x)^3 - 2^3$
$= (3x - 2)(9x^2 + 6x + 4)$

Notes:

3.4 Notetaking with Vocabulary (continued)

The Factor Theorem

A polynomial $f(x)$ has a factor $x - k$ if and only if $f(k) = 0$.

Notes:

Extra Practice

In Exercises 1–14, factor the polynomial completely.

1. $20x^3 - 220x^2 + 600x$

2. $m^5 - 81m$

3. $27a^3 + 8b^3$

4. $5t^6 + 2t^5 - 5t^4 - 2t^3$

5. $y^4 - 13y^2 - 48$

6. $5p^3 + 5p - 5p^2 - 5$

7. $810k^4 - 160$

8. $a^5 + a^3 - a^2 - 1$

3.4 **Notetaking with Vocabulary** (continued)

9. $2x^6 - 8x^5 - 42x^4$

10. $5z^3 + 5z^2 - 6z - 6$

11. $12x^2 - 22x - 20$

12. $3m^2 - 48m^6$

13. $4x^3 - 4x^2 + x$

14. $5m^4 - 70m^3 + 245m^2$

In Exercises 15–17, show that the binomial is a factor of $f(x)$. Then factor $f(x)$ completely.

15. $f(x) = x^3 - 13x - 12;\ x + 1$

16. $f(x) = 6x^3 + 8x^2 - 34x - 12;\ x - 2$

17. $f(x) = 2x^4 - 12x^3 + 6x^2 + 20x;\ x - 5$

3.5 Solving Polynomial Equations
For use with Exploration 3.5

Essential Question How can you determine whether a polynomial equation has a repeated solution?

1 EXPLORATION: Cubic Equations and Repeated Solutions

Work with a partner. Some cubic equations have three distinct solutions. Others have repeated solutions. Match each cubic polynomial equation with the graph of its related polynomial function. Then solve each equation. For those equations that have repeated solutions, describe the behavior of the related function near the repeated zero using the graph or a table of values.

a. $x^3 - 6x^2 + 12x - 8 = 0$ **b.** $x^3 + 3x^2 + 3x + 1 = 0$

c. $x^3 - 3x + 2 = 0$ **d.** $x^3 + x^2 - 2x = 0$

e. $x^3 - 3x - 2 = 0$ **f.** $x^3 - 3x^2 + 2x = 0$

A.

B.

C.

D.

E.

F.

3.5 **Solving Polynomial Equations** (continued)

---

2 **EXPLORATION:** Quartic Equations and Repeated Solutions

Go to *BigIdeasMath.com* for an interactive tool to investigate this exploration.

Work with a partner. Determine whether each quartic equation has repeated solutions using the graph of the related quartic function or a table of values. Explain your reasoning. Then solve each equation.

    a. $x^4 - 4x^3 + 5x^2 - 2x = 0$ **b.** $x^4 - 2x^3 - x^2 + 2x = 0$

    c. $x^4 - 4x^3 + 4x^2 = 0$ **d.** $x^4 + 3x^3 = 0$

Communicate Your Answer

    3. How can you determine whether a polynomial equation has a repeated solution?

    4. Write a cubic or a quartic polynomial equation that is different from the equations in Explorations 1 and 2 and has a repeated solution.

3.5 Notetaking with Vocabulary
For use after Lesson 3.5

In your own words, write the meaning of each vocabulary term.

repeated solution

Core Concepts

The Rational Root Theorem

If $f(x) = a_n x^n + \cdots + a_1 x + a_0$ has *integer* coefficients, then every rational solution of $f(x) = 0$ has the following form:

$$\frac{p}{q} = \frac{\text{factor of constant term } a_0}{\text{factor of leading coefficient } a_n}$$

Notes:

The Irrational Conjugates Theorem

Let f be a polynomial function with rational coefficients, and let a and b be rational numbers such that $\sqrt{b}$ is irrational. If $a + \sqrt{b}$ is a zero of f, then $a - \sqrt{b}$ is also a zero of f.

Notes:

3.5 **Notetaking with Vocabulary** (continued)

Extra Practice

In Exercises 1–6, solve the equation.

1. $36r^3 - r = 0$

2. $20x^3 + 80x^2 = -60x$

3. $3m^2 = 75m^4$

4. $-13y^2 + 36 = -y^4$

5. $2x^3 - x^2 - 2x = -1$

6. $-20c^2 + 50c = 8c^3 - 125$

In Exercises 7–10, find the zeros of the function. Then sketch a graph of the function.

7. $f(x) = x^4 - x^3 - 12x^2$

8. $f(x) = -4x^3 + 12x^2 - 9x$

9. $f(x) = x^3 + 4x^2 - 6x - 24$

10. $f(x) = x^4 - 18x^2 + 81$

3.5 **Notetaking with Vocabulary** (continued)

11. According to the Rational Root Theorem, which is *not* a possible solution of the equation
$2x^4 + 3x^3 - 6x + 7 = 0$?

   A. 3.5   **B.** 0.5   **C.** 7   **D.** 2

12. Find all the real zeros of the function $f(x) = 3x^4 + 11x^3 - 40x^2 - 132x + 48$.

13. Write a polynomial function g of least degree that has rational coefficients, a leading coefficient of 1,
and the zeros -5 and $4 + \sqrt{2}$.

14. Use the information in the graph to answer the questions.

   a. What are the real zeros of the function f?

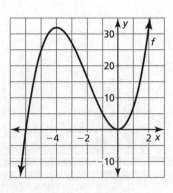

   b. Write an equation of the cubic function in factored form.

3.6 The Fundamental Theorem of Algebra

For use with Exploration 3.6

Essential Question How can you determine whether a polynomial equation has imaginary solutions?

---

1 EXPLORATION: Cubic Equations and Imaginary Solutions

Work with a partner. Match each cubic polynomial equation with the graph of its related polynomial function. Then find *all* solutions. Make a conjecture about how you can use a graph or table of values to determine the number and types of solutions of a cubic polynomial equation.

a. $x^3 - 3x^2 + x + 5 = 0$

b. $x^3 - 2x^2 - x + 2 = 0$

c. $x^3 - x^2 - 4x + 4 = 0$

d. $x^3 + 5x^2 + 8x + 6 = 0$

e. $x^3 - 3x^2 + x - 3 = 0$

f. $x^3 - 3x^2 + 2x = 0$

A.

B.

C.

D.

E.

F.

Integrated Mathematics III
Student Journal   **85**

3.6 **The Fundamental Theorem of Algebra** (continued)

2 **EXPLORATION:** Quartic Equations and Imaginary Solutions

Go to *BigIdeasMath.com* for an interactive tool to investigate this exploration.

Work with a partner. Use the graph of the related quartic function, or a table of values, to determine whether each quartic equation has imaginary solutions. Explain your reasoning. Then find *all* solutions.

a. $x^4 - 2x^3 - x^2 + 2x = 0$

b. $x^4 - 1 = 0$

c. $x^4 + x^3 - x - 1 = 0$

d. $x^4 - 3x^3 + x^2 + 3x - 2 = 0$

Communicate Your Answer

3. How can you determine whether a polynomial equation has imaginary solutions?

4. Is it possible for a cubic equation to have three imaginary solutions? Explain your reasoning.

Name_____ Date_____

Notetaking with Vocabulary
For use after Lesson 3.6

In your own words, write the meaning of each vocabulary term.

complex conjugates

Core Concepts

The Fundamental Theorem of Algebra

Theorem   If $f(x)$ is a polynomial of degree n where $n > 0$, then the equation
$f(x) = 0$ has at least one solution in the set of complex numbers.

Corollary   If $f(x)$ is a polynomial of degree n where $n > 0$, then the equation
$f(x) = 0$ has exactly n solutions provided each solution repeated twice
is counted as two solutions, each solution repeated three times is
counted as three solutions, and so on.

Notes:

3.6 Notetaking with Vocabulary (continued)

The Complex Conjugates Theorem

If f is a polynomial function with real coefficients, and $a + bi$ is an imaginary zero of f, then $a - bi$ is also a zero of f.

Notes:

Descartes's Rule of Signs

Let $f(x) = a_nx^n + a_{n-1}x^{n-1} + \cdots + a_2x^2 + a_1x + a_0$ be a polynomial function with real coefficients.

- The number of *positive real zeros* of f is equal to the number of changes in sign of the coefficients of $f(x)$ or is less than this by an even number.

- The number of *negative real zeros* of f is equal to the number of changes in sign of the coefficients of $f(-x)$ or is less than this by an even number.

Notes:

Name_____ Date _____

Notetaking with Vocabulary (continued)

Extra Practice

In Exercises 1–4, find all zeros of the polynomial function.

1. $h(x) = x^4 - 3x^3 + 6x^2 + 2x - 60$

2. $f(x) = x^3 - 3x^2 - 15x + 125$

3. $g(x) = x^4 - 48x^2 - 49$

4. $h(x) = -5x^3 + 9x^2 - 18x - 4$

In Exercises 5–8, write a polynomial function *f* of least degree that has rational coefficients, a leading coefficient of 1, and the given zeros.

5. $-4, 1, 7$

6. $10, -\sqrt{5}$

7. $8, 3 - i$

8. $0, 2 - \sqrt{2}, 2 + 3i$

Name _____ Date _____

Essential Question How can you transform the graph of a polynomial function?

> **1** **EXPLORATION:** Transforming the Graph of a Cubic Function

Go to *BigIdeasMath.com* for an interactive tool to investigate this exploration.

Work with a partner. The graph of the cubic function

$$f(x) = x^3$$

is shown. The graph of each cubic function g
represents a transformation of the graph of f.
Write a rule for g. Use a graphing calculator
to verify your answers.

a.

b.

c.

d.

3.7 **Transformations of Polynomial Functions** (continued)

---

2 **EXPLORATION:** Transforming the Graph of a Quartic Function

Go to *BigIdeasMath.com* **for an interactive tool to investigate this exploration.**

Work with a partner. The graph of the quartic function

$$f(x) = x^4$$

is shown. The graph of each quartic function g
represents a transformation of the graph of f.
Write a rule for g. Use a graphing calculator
to verify your answers.

a.

b.

Communicate Your Answer

3. How can you transform the graph of a polynomial function?

4. Describe the transformation of $f(x) = x^4$ represented by
   $g(x) = (x + 1)^4 + 3$. Then graph g.

3.7 Notetaking with Vocabulary
For use after Lesson 3.7

In your own words, write the meaning of each vocabulary term.

polynomial function

transformations

Core Concepts

Transformation	$f(x)$ Notation	Examples	
Horizontal Translation Graph shifts left or right.	$f(x-h)$	$g(x) = (x-5)^4$ $g(x) = (x+2)^4$	5 units right 2 units left
Vertical Translation Graph shifts up or down.	$f(x)+k$	$g(x) = x^4 + 1$ $g(x) = x^4 - 4$	1 unit up 4 units down
Reflection Graph flips over x- or y-axis.	$f(-x)$ $-f(x)$	$g(x) = (-x)^4 = x^4$ $g(x) = -x^4$	over y-axis over x-axis
Horizontal Stretch or Shrink Graph stretches away from or shrinks toward y-axis	$f(ax)$	$g(x) = (2x)^4$ $g(x) = \left(\frac{1}{2}x\right)^4$	shrink by a factor of $\frac{1}{2}$ stretch by a factor of 2
Vertical Stretch or Shrink Graph stretches away from or shrinks toward x-axis.	$a \cdot f(x)$	$g(x) = 8x^4$ $g(x) = \frac{1}{4}x^4$	stretch by a factor of 8 shrink by a factor of $\frac{1}{4}$

Notes:

3.7 Notetaking with Vocabulary (continued)

Extra Practice

In Exercises 1–6, describe the transformation of *f* represented by *g*. Then graph each function.

1. $f(x) = x^4$; $g(x) = x^4 - 9$

2. $f(x) = x^5$; $g(x) = (x + 1)^5 + 2$

3. $f(x) = x^6$; $g(x) = -5(x - 2)^6$

4. $f(x) = x^3$; $g(x) = \left(\frac{1}{2}x\right)^3 - 4$

5. $f(x) = x^4$; $g(x) = \frac{1}{8}(-x)^4$

6. $f(x) = x^5$; $g(x) = (x - 10)^5 + 1$

3.7 **Notetaking with Vocabulary** (continued)

7. Graph the function $g(x) = -f(x - 3)$ on the same coordinate plane as $f(x)$.

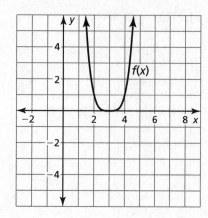

In Exercises 8 and 9, write a rule for *g* and then graph each function. Describe the graph of *g* as a transformation of the graph of *f*.

8. $f(x) = x^3 + 8; g(x) = f(-x) - 9$

9. $f(x) = 2x^5 - x^3 + 1; g(x) = 5f(x)$

In Exercises 10 and 11, write a rule for *g* that represents the indicated transformations of the graph of *f*.

10. $f(x) = x^3 - 6x^2 + 5;$ translation 1 unit left, followed by a reflection in the *x*-axis and a vertical stretch by a factor of 2

11. $f(x) = 3x^4 + x^3 + 3x^2 + 12;$ horizontal shrink by a factor of $\frac{1}{3}$ and a translation 8 units down, followed by a reflection in the *y*-axis

3.8 Analyzing Graphs of Polynomial Functions
For use with Exploration 3.8

Essential Question How many turning points can the graph of a polynomial function have?

1 EXPLORATION: Approximating Turning Points

Go to *BigIdeasMath.com* for an interactive tool to investigate this exploration.

Work with a partner. Match each polynomial function with its graph. Explain your reasoning. Then use a graphing calculator to approximate the coordinates of the turning points of the graph of the function. Round your answers to the nearest hundredth.

a. $f(x) = 2x^2 + 3x - 4$

b. $f(x) = x^2 + 3x + 2$

c. $f(x) = x^3 - 2x^2 - x + 1$

d. $f(x) = -x^3 + 5x - 2$

e. $f(x) = x^4 - 3x^2 + 2x - 1$

f. $f(x) = -2x^5 - x^2 + 5x + 3$

A.

B.

C.

D.

E.

F.

3.8 **Analyzing Graphs of Polynomial Functions** (continued)

Communicate Your Answer

2. How many turning points can the graph of a polynomial function have?

3. Is it possible to sketch the graph of a cubic polynomial function that has *no* turning points? Justify your answer.

Name_____ Date_____

Notetaking with Vocabulary
For use after Lesson 3.8

In your own words, write the meaning of each vocabulary term.

local maximum

local minimum

even function

odd function

Core Concepts

Zeros, Factors, Solutions, and Intercepts

Let $f(x) = a_n x^n + a_{n-1} x^{n-1} + \cdots + a_1 x + a_0$ be a polynomial function. The following statements are equivalent.

Zero: k is a zero of the polynomial function f.

Factor: $x - k$ is a factor of the polynomial $f(x)$.

Solution: k is a solution (or root) of the polynomial equation $f(x) = 0$.

x-Intercept: If k is a real number, then k is an x-intercept of the graph of the polynomial function f. The graph of f passes through $(k, 0)$.

Notes:

3.8   **Notetaking with Vocabulary** (continued)

The Location Principle

If f is a polynomial function, and a and b are two real numbers such that $f(a) < 0$ and $f(b) > 0$, then f has at least one real zero between a and b.

Notes:

Turning Points of Polynomial Functions

1. The graph of every polynomial function of degree n has *at most* $n - 1$ turning points.

2. If a polynomial function has n distinct real zeros, then its graph has *exactly* $n - 1$ turning points.

Notes:

3.8   **Notetaking with Vocabulary** (continued)

Even and Odd Functions

A function f is an **even function** when $f(-x) = f(x)$ for all x in its domain. The graph of an even function is *symmetric about the y-axis*.

A function f is an **odd function** when $f(-x) = -f(x)$ for all x in its domain. The graph of an odd function is *symmetric about the origin*. One way to recognize a graph that is symmetric about the origin is that it looks the same after a $180°$ rotation about the origin.

Even Function

Odd Function

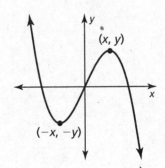

For an even function, if (x, y) is on the graph, then $(-x, y)$ is also on the graph.

For an odd function, if (x, y) is on the graph, then $(-x, -y)$ is also on the graph.

Notes:

3.8 **Notetaking with Vocabulary** (continued)

Extra Practice

In Exercises 1–6, graph the function. Identify the *x*-intercepts, and the points where the local maximums and local minimums occur. Determine the intervals for which the function is increasing or decreasing. Determine whether the function is *even*, *odd*, or *neither*.

1. $f(x) = 4x^3 - 12x^2 - x + 15$

2. $g(x) = 2x^4 + 5x^3 - 21x^2 - 10x$

3. $h(x) = x^3 - x^2 - 13x - 3$

4. $k(x) = x^3 - 2x$

5. $f(x) = x^4 - 29x^2 + 100$

6. $g(x) = -\frac{1}{3}x^3 + x^2 - \frac{4}{3}$

Modeling with Polynomial Functions
For use with Exploration 3.9

Essential Question   How can you find a polynomial model for real-life data?

 EXPLORATION: Modeling Real-Life Data

Go to *BigIdeasMath.com* for an interactive tool to investigate this exploration.

Work with a partner. The distance a baseball travels after it is hit depends on the angle at which it was hit and the initial speed. The table shows the distances a baseball hit at an angle of 35° travels at various initial speeds.

Initial speed, x (miles per hour)	80	85	90	95	100	105	110	115
Distance, y (feet)	194	220	247	275	304	334	365	397

a. Recall that when data have equally-spaced x-values, you can analyze patterns in the differences of the y-values to determine what type of function can be used to model the data. If the first differences are constant, then the set of data fits a linear model. If the second differences are constant, then the set of data fits a quadratic model.

Find the first and second differences of the data. Are the data linear or quadratic? Explain your reasoning.

b. Use a graphing calculator to draw a scatter plot of the data. Do the data appear linear or quadratic? Use the *regression* feature of the graphing calculator to find a linear or quadratic model that best fits the data.

3.9 **Modeling with Polynomial Functions** (continued)

1 **EXPLORATION:** Modeling Real-Life Data (continued)

    c. Use the model you found in part (b) to find the distance a baseball travels when it is hit at an angle of 35° and travels at an initial speed of 120 miles per hour.

    d. According to the *Baseball Almanac,* "Any drive over 400 feet is noteworthy. A blow of 450 feet shows exceptional power, as the majority of major league players are unable to hit a ball that far. Anything in the 500-foot range is genuinely historic." Estimate the initial speed of a baseball that travels a distance of 500 feet.

Communicate Your Answer

    2. How can you find a polynomial model for real-life data?

    3. How well does the model you found in Exploration 1(b) fit the data? Do you think the model is valid for any initial speed? Explain your reasoning.

3.9

Notetaking with Vocabulary
For use after Lesson 3.9

In your own words, write the meaning of each vocabulary term.

finite differences

Core Concepts

Properties of Finite Differences

1. If a polynomial function $y = f(x)$ has degree n, then the nth differences of function values for equally-spaced x-values are nonzero and constant.

2. Conversely, if the nth differences of equally-spaced data are nonzero and constant, then the data can be represented by a polynomial function of degree n.

Notes:

Name _____ Date _____

3.9 Notetaking with Vocabulary (continued)

Extra Practice

In Exercises 1–4, write a cubic function whose graph is shown.

1.

2.

3.

4.

In Exercises 5–8, use finite differences to determine the degree of the polynomial function that fits the data. Then use technology to find the polynomial function.

5.

x	−2	−1	0	1	2	3
f(x)	−14	−6.5	0	5.5	10	13.5

6.

x	−2	−1	0	1	2
f(x)	30	4	0	0	−14

7. $(0, 0), (2, 0), (4, 40), (6, 168),$
   $(8, 432), (10, 880)$

8. $(0, 10), (1, 10), (2, 18), (3, 64),$
   $(4, 202), (5, 510)$

3.9 **Notetaking with Vocabulary** (continued)

9. The table shows the population y of bacteria after x hours. Find a polynomial model for the data for the first 4.5 hours. Use the model to estimate the population level of the bacteria (in thousands) after 1 day.

Number of Hours, x	0.5	1	2.5	3	4	4.5
Number of Bacteria, y	5.125	6	20.625	32	69	96.125

10. The table shows the value y (in thousands of dollars) of a signed autograph of a MVP football player, where x represents the number of years since 2000. Find a polynomial model for the data for the first 5 years. Use the model to estimate the year that the autograph will be valued at $5,000,000?

Number of Years, x	1	2	3	4	5
Value of autograph, y	6	34	162	510	1246

Chapter 4 Maintaining Mathematical Proficiency

Simplify the expression.

1. $c \cdot c^9$

2. $\dfrac{q^{12}}{q^4}$

3. $\dfrac{x^3}{x^4 \cdot x^5}$

4. $\dfrac{d^2}{d} \cdot 8d^5$

5. $\left(\dfrac{4x^3}{2y^4}\right)^2$

6. $\left(\dfrac{m^8 \cdot m^3}{n \cdot m}\right)^3$

Solve the literal equation for y.

7. $x + y = 1$

8. $-3y + \dfrac{1}{2}x = -6$

9. $24x + 5y = 74$

10. $6xy + 3y = -72$

11. $10x - 5xy = 100$

12. $-\dfrac{1}{4}x + 8xy = 16$

13. Is $\left(\dfrac{x + 3x}{y + 2y}\right)^2 = \left(\dfrac{x^2 + 3^2x^2}{y^2 + 2^2y^2}\right)$ or is $\left(\dfrac{x + 3x}{y + 2y}\right)^2 = \left(\dfrac{4^2x^2}{3^2y^2}\right)$? Explain your

reasoning.

4.1 *n*th Roots and Rational Exponents

For use with Exploration 4.1

Essential Question How can you use a rational exponent to represent a power involving a radical?

---

1 **EXPLORATION:** Exploring the Definition of a Rational Exponent

Work with a partner. Use a calculator to show that each statement is true.

a. $\sqrt{9} = 9^{1/2}$

b. $\sqrt{2} = 2^{1/2}$

c. $\sqrt[3]{8} = 8^{1/3}$

d. $\sqrt[3]{3} = 3^{1/3}$

e. $\sqrt[4]{16} = 16^{1/4}$

f. $\sqrt[4]{12} = 12^{1/4}$

---

2 **EXPLORATION:** Writing Expressions in Rational Exponent Form

Work with a partner. Use the definition of a rational exponent and the properties of exponents to write each expression as a base with a single rational exponent. Then use a calculator to evaluate each expression. Round your answer to two decimal places.

Sample

$$\left(\sqrt[3]{4}\right)^2 = \left(4^{1/3}\right)^2$$
$$= 4^{2/3}$$
$$\approx 2.52$$

```
4^(2/3)
                 2.5198421
```

a. $\left(\sqrt{5}\right)^3$

b. $\left(\sqrt[4]{4}\right)^2$

c. $\left(\sqrt[3]{9}\right)^2$

d. $\left(\sqrt[5]{10}\right)^4$

e. $\left(\sqrt{15}\right)^3$

f. $\left(\sqrt[3]{27}\right)^4$

4.1 *n*th Roots and Rational Exponents (continued)

---

3 **EXPLORATION:** Writing Expressions in Radical Form

Work with a partner. Use the properties of exponents and the definition of a rational exponent to write each expression as a radical raised to an exponent. Then use a calculator to evaluate each expression. Round your answer to two decimal places.

Sample $5^{2/3} = \left(5^{1/3}\right)^2 = \left(\sqrt[3]{5}\right)^2 \approx 2.92$

    a. $8^{2/3}$ **b.** $6^{5/2}$ **c.** $12^{3/4}$

    d. $10^{3/2}$ **e.** $16^{3/2}$ **f.** $20^{6/5}$

Communicate Your Answer

4. How can you use a rational exponent to represent a power involving a radical?

5. Evaluate each expression *without* using a calculator. Explain your reasoning.

    a. $4^{3/2}$ **b.** $32^{4/5}$ **c.** $625^{3/4}$

    d. $49^{3/2}$ **e.** $125^{4/3}$ **f.** $100^{6/3}$

4.1 Notetaking with Vocabulary
For use after Lesson 4.1

In your own words, write the meaning of each vocabulary term.

nth root of a

index of a radical

Core Concepts

Real nth roots of a

Let n be an integer $(n > 1)$ and let a be a real number.

n is an even integer.	n is an odd integer.
$a < 0$ No real nth roots	$a < 0$ One real nth root: $\sqrt[n]{a} = a^{1/n}$
$a = 0$ One real nth root: $\sqrt[n]{0} = 0$	$a = 0$ One real nth root: $\sqrt[n]{0} = 0$
$a > 0$ Two real nth roots: $\pm\sqrt[n]{a} = \pm a^{1/n}$	$a > 0$ One real nth root: $\sqrt[n]{a} = a^{1/n}$

Notes:

4.1 **Notetaking with Vocabulary** (continued)

Rational Exponents

Let $a^{1/n}$ be an nth root of a, and let m be a positive integer.

$$a^{m/n} = \left(a^{1/n}\right)^m = \left(\sqrt[n]{a}\right)^m$$

$$a^{-m/n} = \frac{1}{a^{m/n}} = \frac{1}{\left(a^{1/n}\right)^m} = \frac{1}{\left(\sqrt[n]{a}\right)^m}, a \neq 0$$

Notes:

Extra Practice

In Exercises 1–3, find the indicated real nth root(s) of a.

1. $n = 3, a = -125$

2. $n = 2, a = -400$

3. $n = 6, a = 64$

In Exercises 4–11, evaluate the expression without using a calculator.

4. $64^{1/2}$

5. $(-27)^{1/3}$

6. $32^{7/5}$

7. $49^{-3/2}$

8. $(-32)^{3/5}$

9. $1000^{-2/3}$

10. $81^{3/4}$

11. $625^{1/4}$

4.1 Notetaking with Vocabulary (continued)

In Exercises 12–15, match the equivalent expressions. Explain your reasoning.

12. $\left(\sqrt{a}\right)^3$

    A. $a^{-1/3}$

13. $-\sqrt[3]{a}$

    B. $a^{2/3}$

14. $\left(\sqrt[3]{a}\right)^2$

    C. $a^{3/2}$

15. $\dfrac{1}{\sqrt[3]{a}}$

    D. $-a^{1/3}$

In Exercises 16–19, find the real solution(s) of the equation. Round your answer to two decimal places when appropriate.

16. $6x^3 = -6$

17. $2(x+5)^4 = 128$

18. $x^5 - 32 = -64$

19. $-\dfrac{1}{10}x^3 + 100 = 0$

20. The volume of a cube is 1728 cubic inches. What are the dimensions of the cube?

Name _____ Date _____

Properties of Rational Exponents and Radicals
For use with Exploration 4.2

Essential Question How can you use properties of exponents to simplify products and quotients of radicals?

1 EXPLORATION: Reviewing Properties of Exponents

Work with a partner. Let a and b be real numbers. Use the properties of exponents to complete each statement. Then match each completed statement with the property it illustrates.

Statement	Property
a. $a^{-2} = $_____, $a \neq 0$	**A.** Product of Powers
b. $(ab)^4 = $_____	**B.** Power of a Power
c. $(a^3)^4 = $_____	**C.** Power of a Product
d. $a^3 \cdot a^4 = $_____	**D.** Negative Exponent
e. $\left(\dfrac{a}{b}\right)^3 = $_____, $b \neq 0$	**E.** Zero Exponent
f. $\dfrac{a^6}{a^2} = $_____, $a \neq 0$	**F.** Quotient of Powers
g. $a^0 = $_____, $a \neq 0$	**G.** Power of a Quotient

2 EXPLORATION: Simplifying Expressions with Rational Exponents

Work with a partner. Show that you can apply the properties of integer exponents to rational exponents by simplifying each expression. Use a calculator to check your answers.

a. $5^{2/3} \cdot 5^{4/3}$ **b.** $3^{1/5} \cdot 3^{4/5}$ **c.** $\left(4^{2/3}\right)^3$

d. $\left(10^{1/2}\right)^4$ **e.** $\dfrac{8^{5/2}}{8^{1/2}}$ **f.** $\dfrac{7^{2/3}}{7^{5/3}}$

4.2 **Properties of Rational Exponents and Radicals** (continued)

---

3 **EXPLORATION:** Simplifying Products and Quotients of Radicals

Work with a partner. Use the properties of exponents to write each expression as a single radical. Then evaluate each expression. Use a calculator to check your answers.

a. $\sqrt{3} \cdot \sqrt{12}$ b. $\sqrt[3]{5} \cdot \sqrt[3]{25}$ c. $\sqrt[4]{27} \cdot \sqrt[4]{3}$

d. $\dfrac{\sqrt{98}}{\sqrt{2}}$ e. $\dfrac{\sqrt[4]{4}}{\sqrt[4]{1024}}$ f. $\dfrac{\sqrt[3]{625}}{\sqrt[3]{5}}$

Communicate Your Answer

4. How can you use properties of exponents to simplify products and quotients of radicals?

5. Simplify each expression.

a. $\sqrt{27} \cdot \sqrt{6}$ b. $\dfrac{\sqrt[3]{240}}{\sqrt[3]{15}}$ c. $\left(5^{1/2} \cdot 16^{1/4}\right)^{2}$

4.2 Notetaking with Vocabulary
For use after Lesson 4.2

In your own words, write the meaning of each vocabulary term.

simplest form of a radical

conjugate

like radicals

Core Concepts

Properties of Rational Exponents

Let a and b be real numbers and let m and n be rational numbers, such that the quantities in each property are real numbers.

Property Name	Definition	Example
Product of Powers	$a^m \cdot a^n = a^{m+n}$	$5^{1/2} \cdot 5^{3/2} = 5^{(1/2+3/2)} = 5^2 = 25$
Power of a Power	$\left(a^m\right)^n = a^{mn}$	$\left(3^{5/2}\right)^2 = 3^{(5/2 \cdot 2)} = 3^5 = 243$
Power of a Product	$(ab)^m = a^m b^m$	$(16 \cdot 9)^{1/2} = 16^{1/2} \cdot 9^{1/2} = 4 \cdot 3 = 12$
Negative Exponent	$a^{-m} = \dfrac{1}{a^m}, a \neq 0$	$36^{-1/2} = \dfrac{1}{36^{1/2}} = \dfrac{1}{6}$
Zero Exponent	$a^0 = 1, a \neq 0$	$213^0 = 1$
Quotient of Powers	$\dfrac{a^m}{a^n} = a^{m-n}, a \neq 0$	$\dfrac{4^{5/2}}{4^{1/2}} = 4^{(5/2-1/2)} = 4^2 = 16$
Power of a Quotient	$\left(\dfrac{a}{b}\right)^m = \dfrac{a^m}{b^m}, b \neq 0$	$\left(\dfrac{27}{64}\right)^{1/3} = \dfrac{27^{1/3}}{64^{1/3}} = \dfrac{3}{4}$

Notes:

Name_____ Date_____

Properties of Radicals

Let a and b be real numbers and let n be an integer greater than 1.

Property Name	Definition	Example
Product Property	$\sqrt[n]{a \bullet b} = \sqrt[n]{a} \bullet \sqrt[n]{b}$	$\sqrt[3]{4} \bullet \sqrt[3]{2} = \sqrt[3]{8} = 2$
Quotient Property	$\sqrt[n]{\dfrac{a}{b}} = \dfrac{\sqrt[n]{a}}{\sqrt[n]{b}}, b \neq 0$	$\dfrac{\sqrt[4]{162}}{\sqrt[4]{2}} = \sqrt[4]{\dfrac{162}{2}} = \sqrt[4]{81} = 3$

Notes:

Extra Practice

In Exercises 1–4, use the properties of rational exponents to simplify the expression.

1. $\left(2^3 \bullet 3^3\right)^{-1/3}$

2. $\dfrac{10}{10^{-4/5}}$

3. $\left(\dfrac{52^5}{4^5}\right)^{1/6}$

4. $\dfrac{3^{1/3} \bullet 27^{2/3}}{8^{4/3}}$

5. Find simplified expressions for the perimeter and area of the given figure.

$10x^{1/4}$

Name _____ Date _____

In Exercises 6–8, use the properties of radicals to simplify the expression.

6. $\sqrt[6]{25} \cdot \sqrt[6]{625}$

7. $\dfrac{\sqrt{343}}{\sqrt{7}}$

8. $\dfrac{\sqrt[3]{25} \cdot \sqrt[3]{10}}{\sqrt[3]{2}}$

In Exercises 9–12, write the expression in simplest form.

9. $\sqrt[7]{384}$

10. $\sqrt[3]{\dfrac{5}{9}}$

11. $\dfrac{1}{4 - \sqrt{5}}$

12. $\dfrac{\sqrt{2}}{1 + \sqrt{6}}$

In Exercises 13–16, write the expression in simplest form. Assume all variables are positive.

13. $-2\sqrt[3]{5} + 40\sqrt[3]{5}$

14. $2(1250)^{1/4} - 5(32)^{1/4}$

15. $\dfrac{\sqrt[4]{x} \cdot \sqrt[4]{81x}}{\sqrt[4]{16x^{36}}}$

16. $\dfrac{21\left(x^{-3/2}\right)\left(\sqrt{y}\right)\left(z^{5/2}\right)}{7^{-1}\sqrt{x}\left(y^{-1/2}\right)z}$

Name_____ Date_____

4.3 Graphing Radical Functions
For use with Exploration 4.3

Essential Question How can you identify the domain and range of a radical function?

1 EXPLORATION: Identifying Graphs of Radical Functions

Work with a partner. Match each function with its graph. Explain your reasoning. Then identify the domain and range of each function.

a. $f(x) = \sqrt{x}$

b. $f(x) = \sqrt[3]{x}$

c. $f(x) = \sqrt[4]{x}$

d. $f(x) = \sqrt[5]{x}$

A.

B.

C.

D.

4.3 Graphing Radical Functions (continued)

---

2 **EXPLORATION:** Identifying Graphs of Transformations

Work with a partner. Match each transformation of $f(x) = \sqrt{x}$ with its graph.
Explain your reasoning. Then identify the domain and range of each function.

    a. $g(x) = \sqrt{x + 2}$ **b.** $g(x) = \sqrt{x - 2}$

    c. $g(x) = \sqrt{x + 2} - 2$ **d.** $g(x) = -\sqrt{x + 2}$

A.   **B.**

C.   **D.**

Communicate Your Answer

    3. How can you identify the domain and range of a radical function?

    4. Use the results of Exploration 1 to describe how the domain and range of a radical
         function are related to the index of the radical.

Name_____ Date _____

Notetaking with Vocabulary
For use after Lesson 4.3

In your own words, write the meaning of each vocabulary term.

radical function

Core Concepts

Parent Functions for Square Root and Cube Root Functions

The parent function for the family of square root functions is $f(x) = \sqrt{x}$.

Domain: $x \geq 0$, Range: $y \geq 0$

The parent function for the family of cube root functions is $f(x) = \sqrt[3]{x}$.

Domain and range: All real numbers

Notes:

4.3 Notetaking with Vocabulary (continued)

Transformation	$f(x)$ Notation	Examples	
Horizontal Translation Graph shifts left or right.	$f(x - h)$	$g(x) = \sqrt{x - 2}$ $g(x) = \sqrt{x + 3}$	2 units right 3 units left
Vertical Translation Graph shifts up or down.	$f(x) + k$	$g(x) = \sqrt{x} + 7$ $g(x) = \sqrt{x} - 1$	7 units up 1 unit down
Reflection Graph flips over x- or y-axis.	$f(-x)$ $-f(x)$	$g(x) = \sqrt{-x}$ $g(x) = -\sqrt{x}$	in the y-axis in the x-axis
Horizontal Stretch or Shrink Graph stretches away from or shrinks toward y-axis.	$f(ax)$	$g(x) = \sqrt{3x}$ $g(x) = \sqrt{\frac{1}{2}x}$	shrink by a factor of $\frac{1}{3}$ stretch by a factor of 2
Vertical Stretch or Shrink Graph stretches away from or shrinks toward x-axis.	$a \bullet f(x)$	$g(x) = 4\sqrt{x}$ $g(x) = \frac{1}{5}\sqrt{x}$	stretch by a factor of 4 shrink by a factor of $\frac{1}{5}$

Notes:

Name_____ Date_____

Extra Practice

In Exercises 1 and 2, graph the function. Identify the domain and range of each function.

1. $f(x) = \sqrt[3]{-3x} + 1$

2. $g(x) = 2(x - 5)^{1/2} - 4$

3. Describe the transformation of $f(x) = \sqrt[4]{2x} + 5$ represented by $g(x) = -\sqrt[4]{2x} - 5$.

4. Write a rule for g if g is a horizontal shrink by a factor of $\frac{5}{6}$, followed by a translation 10 units to the left of the graph of $f(x) = \sqrt[3]{15x + 1}$.

5. Use a graphing calculator to graph $8x = y^2 + 5$.
   Identify the vertex and the direction that the parabola opens.

6. Use a graphing calculator to graph $x^2 = 49 - y^2$.
   Identify the center, radius, and intercepts of the circle.

Solving Radical Equations and Inequalities

For use with Exploration 4.4

Essential Question How can you solve a radical equation?

1 **EXPLORATION:** Solving Radical Equations

Work with a partner. Match each radical equation with the graph of its related radical function. Explain your reasoning. Then use the graph to solve the equation, if possible. Check your solutions.

a. $\sqrt{x-1} - 1 = 0$ b. $\sqrt{2x+2} - \sqrt{x+4} = 0$ c. $\sqrt{9-x^2} = 0$

d. $\sqrt{x+2} - x = 0$ e. $\sqrt{-x+2} - x = 0$ f. $\sqrt{3x^2+1} = 0$

A.

B.

C.

D.

E.

F.

4.4 **Solving Radical Equations and Inequalities** (continued)

---

2 **EXPLORATION:** Solving Radical Equations

Go to *BigIdeasMath.com* **for an interactive tool to investigate this exploration.**

Work with a partner. Look back at the radical equations in Exploration 1. Suppose that you did not know how to solve the equations using a graphical approach.

   a. Show how you could use a *numerical approach* to solve one of the equations. For instance, you might use a spreadsheet to create a table of values.

   b. Show how you could use an *analytical approach* to solve one of the equations. For instance, look at the similarities between the equations in Exploration 1. What first step may be necessary so you could square each side to eliminate the radical(s)? How would you proceed to find the solution?

Communicate Your Answer

   3. How can you solve a radical equation?

   4. Would you prefer to use a graphical, numerical, or analytical approach to solve the given equation? Explain your reasoning. Then solve the equation.

$$\sqrt{x + 3} - \sqrt{x - 2} = 1$$

4.4 Notetaking with Vocabulary
For use after Lesson 4.4

In your own words, write the meaning of each vocabulary term.

radical equation

extraneous solutions

Core Concepts

Solving Radical Equations

To solve a radical equation, follow these steps:

Step 1 Isolate the radical on one side of the equation, if necessary.

Step 2 Raise each side of the equation to the same exponent to eliminate the radical and obtain a linear, quadratic, or other polynomial equation.

Step 3 Solve the resulting equation using techniques you learned previously. Check your solution.

Notes:

4.4 **Notetaking with Vocabulary** (continued)

Extra Practice

In Exercises 1–10, solve the equation. Check your solution(s).

1. $\sqrt{1-x} = 7$

2. $\sqrt[3]{5x+1} = -4$

3. $\frac{1}{4}\sqrt[4]{2x} + 6 = 10$

4. $2\sqrt[3]{13x-5} = 10$

5. $x - 7 = \sqrt{x-5}$

6. $\sqrt[3]{486 - 27x^3} = 3x$

7. $4\sqrt{x+1} = x + 1$

8. $\sqrt{2x+2} - 3\sqrt{x+1} = 0$

9. $2 - \sqrt[4]{2x-6} = 14$

10. $\sqrt{x+7} + 2 = \sqrt{3-x}$

4.4 **Notetaking with Vocabulary** (continued)

In Exercises 11 and 12, solve the equation. Check your solution(s).

11. $\frac{1}{2}x^{5/2} = 16$

12. $(6x + 10)^{7/3} + 28 = 156$

In Exercises 13–15, solve the inequality.

13. $-4\sqrt{x - 1} + 3 \geq -1$

14. $\sqrt[3]{\frac{2}{3}x + 1} < 6$

15. $2\sqrt{\frac{3}{4}x} - 39 \leq -25$

16. In basketball, the term "hang time" is the amount of time that a player is suspended in the air when making a basket. To win a slam-dunk contest, players try to maximize their hang time. A player's hang time is given by the equation $t = 0.5\sqrt{h}$, where t is the time (in seconds) and h is the height (in feet) of the jump. The second-place finisher of a slam-dunk contest had a hang time of 1 second, and the winner had a hang time of 1.2 seconds. How many feet higher did the winner jump than the second-place finisher?

4.5 Performing Function Operations

For use with Exploration 4.5

Essential Question How can you use the graphs of two functions to sketch the graph of an arithmetic combination of the two functions?

Just as two real numbers can be combined by the operations of addition, subtraction, multiplication, and division to form other real numbers, two functions can be combined to form other functions. For example, the functions $f(x) = 2x - 3$ and $g(x) = x^2 - 1$ can be combined to form the sum, difference, product, or quotient of f and g.

$$f(x) + g(x) = (2x - 3) + (x^2 - 1) = x^2 + 2x - 4 \qquad \text{sum}$$

$$f(x) - g(x) = (2x - 3) - (x^2 - 1) = -x^2 + 2x - 2 \qquad \text{difference}$$

$$f(x) \bullet g(x) = (2x - 3)(x^2 - 1) = 2x^3 - 3x^2 - 2x + 3 \qquad \text{product}$$

$$\frac{f(x)}{g(x)} = \frac{2x - 3}{x^2 - 1} \qquad \text{quotient}$$

---

1 EXPLORATION: Graphing the Sum of Two Functions

Go to *BigIdeasMath.com* for an interactive tool to investigate this exploration.

Work with a partner. Use the graphs of f and g to sketch the graph of $f + g$. Explain your steps.

Sample Choose a point on the graph of g. Use a compass or a ruler to measure its distance above or below the x-axis. If above, add the distance to the y-coordinate of the point with the same x-coordinate of the graph of f. If below, subtract the distance. Plot the new point. Repeat this process for several points. Finally, draw a smooth curve through the new points to obtain the graph of $f + g$.

4.5 **Performing Function Operations** (continued)

---

1 **EXPLORATION:** Graphing the Sum of Two Functions (continued)

a.

b.
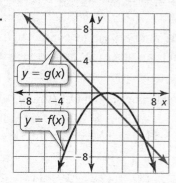

Communicate Your Answer

2. How can you use the graphs of two functions to sketch the graph of an arithmetic combination of the two functions?

3. Check your answers in Exploration 1 by writing equations for *f* and *g*, adding the functions, and graphing the sum.

Name_____ Date_____

4.5   Notetaking with Vocabulary
For use after Lesson 4.5

In your own words, write the meaning of each vocabulary term.

domain

scientific notation

Core Concepts

Operations on Functions

Let f and g be any two functions. A new function can be defined by performing any of the four basic operations on f and g.

Operation	Definition	Example: $f(x) = 5x$, $g(x) = x + 2$
Addition	$(f + g)(x) = f(x) + g(x)$	$(f + g)(x) = 5x + (x + 2) = 6x + 2$
Subtraction	$(f - g)(x) = f(x) - g(x)$	$(f - g)(x) = 5x - (x + 2) = 4x - 2$
Multiplication	$(fg)(x) = f(x) \cdot g(x)$	$(fg)(x) = 5x(x + 2) = 5x^2 + 10x$
Division	$\left(\dfrac{f}{g}\right)(x) = \dfrac{f(x)}{g(x)}$	$\left(\dfrac{f}{g}\right)(x) = \dfrac{5x}{x + 2}$

The domains of the sum, difference, product, and quotient functions consist of the x-values that are in the domains of both f and g. Additionally, the domain of the quotient does not include x-values for which $g(x) = 0$.

Notes:

4.5 Notetaking with Vocabulary (continued)

Extra Practice

In Exercises 1–4, find $(f + g)(x)$ and $(f - g)(x)$ and state the domain of each. Then evaluate $f + g$ and $f - g$ for the given value of x.

1. $f(x) = -\frac{1}{2}\sqrt[3]{x}, g(x) = \frac{9}{2}\sqrt[3]{x}; x = -1000$

2. $f(x) = -x^2 - 3x + 8, g(x) = 6x - 3x^2; x = -1$

3. $f(x) = 4x^3 + 12, g(x) = 2x^2 - 3x^3 + 9; x = 2$

4. $f(x) = 5\sqrt[4]{x} + 1, g(x) = -3\sqrt[4]{x} - 2; x = 1$

In Exercises 5–8, find $(fg)(x)$ and $\left(\dfrac{f}{g}\right)(x)$ and state the domain of each. Then evaluate fg and $\dfrac{f}{g}$ for the given value of x.

5. $f(x) = -x^3, g(x) = 2\sqrt[3]{x}; x = -64$ 6. $f(x) = 12x, g(x) = 11x^{1/2}; x = 4$

7. $f(x) = 0.25x^{1/3}, g(x) = -4x^{3/2}; x = 1$ 8. $f(x) = 36x^{7/4}, g(x) = 4x^{1/2}; x = 16$

4.5 Notetaking with Vocabulary (continued)

9. The graphs of the functions $f(x) = x^2 - 4x + 4$ and $g(x) = 4x - 5$ are shown. Which graph represents the function $f + g$? the function $f - g$? Explain your reasoning.

$f(x) = x^2 - 4x + 4$

$g(x) = 4x - 5$

A.

$y = x^2 - 8x + 9$

B.

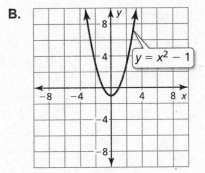

$y = x^2 - 1$

10. The variable x represents the number of pages of a textbook to be printed. The cost C to print the textbook can be modeled by the equation $C(x) = 0.2x^2 + 10$. The selling price P of the textbook can be modeled by the equation $P(x) = 0.05x^2 + 20$.

a. Find $(P - C)(x)$.

b. Explain what $(P - C)(x)$ represents.

Name _____ Date _____

Essential Question How can you sketch the graph of the inverse of a function?

---

1 EXPLORATION: Graphing Functions and Their Inverses

Go to *BigIdeasMath.com* for an interactive tool to investigate this exploration.

Work with a partner. Each pair of functions are *inverses* of each other. Use a graphing calculator to graph f and g in the same viewing window. What do you notice about the graphs?

a. $f(x) = 4x + 3$

$g(x) = \dfrac{x - 3}{4}$

b. $f(x) = x^3 + 1$

$g(x) = \sqrt[3]{x - 1}$

c. $f(x) = \sqrt{x - 3}$

$g(x) = x^2 + 3, x \geq 0$

d. $f(x) = -\sqrt{x} + 2$

$g(x) = (2 - x)^2, x \leq 2$

4.6 **Inverse of a Function** (continued)

---

2 **EXPLORATION:** Sketching Graphs of Inverse Functions

Go to *BigIdeasMath.com* for an interactive tool to investigate this exploration.

Work with a partner. Use the graph of f to sketch the graph of g, the inverse function of f, on the same set of coordinate axes. Explain your reasoning.

a.

b.

c.

d.

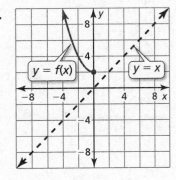

Communicate Your Answer

3. How can you sketch the graph of the inverse of a function?

4. In Exploration 1, what do you notice about the relationship between the equations of f and g? Use your answer to find g, the inverse function of

$$f(x) = 2x - 3.$$

Use a graph to check your answer.

4.6 Notetaking with Vocabulary
For use after Lesson 4.6

In your own words, write the meaning of each vocabulary term.

inverse functions

Core Concepts

Horizontal Line Test

The inverse of a function *f* is also a function if and only if no horizontal line intersects the graph of *f* more than once.

Inverse is a function

Inverse is not a function

Notes:

Name_____ Date_____

Extra Practice

In Exercises 1–3, solve $y = f(x)$ for x. Then find the input(s) when the output is -6.

1. $f(x) = 2x - 1$

2. $f(x) = 1 - x^2$

3. $f(x) = (x - 1)^3 + 2$

In Exercises 4–6, find the inverse of the function. Then graph the function and its inverse.

4. $f(x) = 10x$

5. $f(x) = -\frac{1}{5}x - 7$

6. $f(x) = \frac{3}{4}x + \frac{5}{8}$

In Exercises 7 and 8, determine whether each pair of functions f and g are inverses. Explain your reasoning.

7.

x	−4	−3	−2	−1	0	1
f(x)	17	13	9	5	1	−3

x	17	13	9	5	1	−3
g(x)	−4	−3	−2	−1	0	1

8.

x	1	2	3	4	5	6
f(x)	−1	−2	−4	−5	−8	−10

x	−1	−0.5	−0.25	−0.2	−0.125	−0.1
g(x)	1	2	3	4	5	6

Name _____ Date _____

In Exercises 9 and 10, find the inverse of the function. Then graph the function and its inverse.

9. $f(x) = (x + 2)^3$

10. $f(x) = \frac{1}{3}x^4, x \ge 0$

In Exercises 11 and 12, use the graph to determine whether the inverse of f is a function. Explain your reasoning.

11.

12.

In Exercises 13 and 14, determine whether the functions are inverse functions.

13. $f(x) = \frac{4x}{5} - 1, g(x) = \frac{5x + 1}{4}$

14. $f(x) = -(x - 2)^5 + 6, g(x) = 2 + (6 - x)^{1/5}$

Chapter 5   Maintaining Mathematical Proficiency

Evaluate the expression.

1. $-4 \cdot 5^3$ **2.** $(-3)^4$ **3.** $-\left(\frac{7}{8}\right)^2$ **4.** $\left(\frac{3}{10}\right)^3$

Tell whether the function represents *exponential growth* or *exponential decay*. Then graph the function.

5. $f(x) = 0.5^x$ **6.** $y = 4^x$

7. $g(x) = 2.6^x$ **8.** $h(x) = 0.25^x$

9. Is the expression "the sum of the square of x and the square of the opposite of x" equivalent to 0 or $2x^2$? Explain your reasoning.

Name _____ Date _____

Essential Question   What is the natural base *e*?

So far in your study of mathematics, you have worked with special numbers such as π and i. Another special number is called the *natural base* and is denoted by *e*. The natural base *e* is irrational, so you cannot find its exact value.

---

1 EXPLORATION: Approximating the Natural Base *e*

Go to *BigIdeasMath.com* for an interactive tool to investigate this exploration.

Work with a partner. One way to approximate the natural base *e* is to approximate the sum

$$1 + \frac{1}{1} + \frac{1}{1 \bullet 2} + \frac{1}{1 \bullet 2 \bullet 3} + \frac{1}{1 \bullet 2 \bullet 3 \bullet 4} + \cdots.$$

Use a spreadsheet or a graphing calculator to approximate this sum. Explain the steps you used. How many decimal places did you use in your approximation?

---

2 EXPLORATION: Approximating the Natural Base *e*

Work with a partner. Another way to approximate the natural base *e* is to consider the expression

$$\left(1 + \frac{1}{x}\right)^{x}.$$

As *x* increases, the value of this expression approaches the value of *e*. Complete the table. Then use the results in the table to approximate *e*. Compare this approximation to the one you obtained in Exploration 1.

x	10^1	10^2	10^3	10^4	10^5	10^6
$\left(1 + \dfrac{1}{x}\right)^{x}$						

5.1 **The Natural Base e** (continued)

3 **EXPLORATION:** Graphing a Natural Base Function

Go to *BigIdeasMath.com* for an interactive tool to investigate this exploration.

Work with a partner. Use your approximate value of e in Exploration 1 or 2 to complete the table. Then sketch the graph of the *natural base exponential function* $y = e^x$. You can use a graphing calculator and the $\boxed{e^x}$ key to check your graph. What are the domain and range of $y = e^x$? Justify your answers.

x	-2	-1	0	1	2
$y = e^x$					

Communicate Your Answer

4. What is the natural base e?

5. Repeat Exploration 3 for the natural base exponential function $y = e^{-x}$. Then compare the graph of $y = e^x$ to the graph of $y = e^{-x}$.

x	-2	-1	0	1	2
$y = e^{-x}$					

6. The natural base e is used in a wide variety of real-life applications. Use the Internet or some other reference to research some of the real-life applications of e.

5.1 Notetaking with Vocabulary
For use after Lesson 5.1

In your own words, write the meaning of each vocabulary term.

natural base e

Core Concepts

The Natural Base e

The natural base e is irrational. It is defined as follows:

As x approaches $+\infty$, $\left(1 + \dfrac{1}{x}\right)^x$ approaches $e \approx 2.71828182846$.

Notes:

Natural Base Functions

A function of the form $y = ae^{rx}$ is called a *natural base exponential function*.

- When $a > 0$ and $r > 0$, the function is an exponential growth function.

- When $a > 0$ and $r < 0$, the function is an exponential decay function.

The graphs of the basic functions $y = e^x$ and $y = e^{-x}$ are shown.

Notes:

Name_____ Date _____

Continuously Compounded Interest

When interest is compounded *continuously*, the amount A in an account after t years is given by the formula

$$A = Pe^{rt}$$

where P is the principal and r is the annual interest rate expressed as a decimal.

Notes:

Extra Practice

In Exercises 1–4, simplify the expression.

1. $e^{-9} \cdot e^{12}$ **2.** $\dfrac{25e^2}{35e^7}$ **3.** $\left(2e^{-3x}\right)^5 \cdot 2e^{x+1}$ **4.** $\sqrt[4]{16e^{24x}}$

In Exercises 5–8, tell whether the function represents *exponential growth* or *exponential decay*. Then graph the function.

5. $y = 2e^{-x}$ **6.** $y = 0.75e^{4x}$ **7.** $y = 5e^{0.25x}$ **8.** $y = 0.8e^{-3x}$

5.1 **Notetaking with Vocabulary** (continued)

In Exercises 9–11, use a table of values or a graphing calculator to graph the function. Then identify the domain and range.

9. $y = e^x - 4$ **10.** $y = 2e^{x+3}$ **11.** $y = -e^x + 5$

12. The population of Evans City is currently 48,500 and is declining at a rate of 2.5% each year. You can model the population of Evans City by the equation $P_t = P_c e^{rt}$, where P_c is the current population, P_t is the population after t years, and r is the decimal rate of decline per year. Predict the population of Evans City after 25 years.

13. Your parents will need $25,000 in 10 years to pay for your brother's college tuition. They can invest in an account with an interest rate of 9.8% that compounds continuously. How much should your parents invest today in order to have your brother's full tuition available in 10 years?

5.2 Logarithms and Logarithmic Functions
For use with Exploration 5.2

Essential Question What are some of the characteristics of the graph of a logarithmic function?

Every exponential function of the form $f(x) = b^x$, where b is a positive real number other than 1, has an inverse function that you can denote by $g(x) = \log_b x$. This inverse function is called a *logarithmic function with base b*.

---

1 EXPLORATION: Rewriting Exponential Equations

Work with a partner. Find the value of x in each exponential equation. Explain your reasoning. Then use the value of x to rewrite the exponential equation in its equivalent logarithmic form, $x = \log_b y$.

a. $2^x = 8$ **b.** $3^x = 9$ **c.** $4^x = 2$

d. $5^x = 1$ **e.** $5^x = \dfrac{1}{5}$ **f.** $8^x = 4$

---

2 EXPLORATION: Graphing Exponential and Logarithmic Functions

Go to *BigIdeasMath.com* for an interactive tool to investigate this exploration.

Work with a partner. Complete each table for the given exponential function. Use the results to complete the table for the given logarithmic function. Explain your reasoning. Then sketch the graphs of f and g in the same coordinate plane.

a.

x	−2	−1	0	1	2
$f(x) = 2^x$					

x					
$g(x) = \log_2 x$	−2	−1	0	1	2

Name _____ Date _____

2 **EXPLORATION:** Graphing Exponential and Logarithmic Functions (continued)

b.

x	−2	−1	0	1	2
$f(x) = 10^x$					

x					
$g(x) = \log_{10} x$	−2	−1	0	1	2

3 **EXPLORATION:** Characteristics of Graphs of Logarithmic Functions

Work with a partner. Use the graphs you sketched in Exploration 2 to determine the domain, range, x-intercept, and asymptote of the graph of $g(x) = \log_b x$, where b is a positive real number other than 1. Explain your reasoning.

Communicate Your Answer

4. What are some of the characteristics of the graph of a logarithmic function?

5. How can you use the graph of an exponential function to obtain the graph of a logarithmic function?

5.2 Notetaking with Vocabulary
For use after Lesson 5.2

In your own words, write the meaning of each vocabulary term.

logarithm of y with base b

common logarithm

natural logarithm

Core Concepts

Definition of Logarithm with Base b

Let b and y be positive real numbers with $b \neq 1$. The **logarithm of y with base b** is denoted by $\log_b y$ and is defined as

$$\log_b y = x \qquad \text{if and only if} \qquad b^x = y.$$

The expression $\log_b y$ is read as "log base b of y."

Notes:

5.2 Notetaking with Vocabulary (continued)

Parent Graphs for Logarithmic Functions

The graph of $f(x) = \log_b x$ is shown below for $b > 1$ and for $0 < b < 1$.

Because $f(x) = \log_b x$ and $g(x) = b^x$ are inverse functions, the graph of

$f(x) = \log_b x$ is the reflection of the graph of $g(x) = b^x$ in the line $y = x$.

Graph of $f(x) = \log_b x$ for $b > 1$ Graph of $f(x) = \log_b x$ for $0 < b < 1$

Note that the y-axis is a vertical asymptote of the graph of $f(x) = \log_b x$. The domain of

$f(x) = \log_b x$ is $x > 0$, and the range is all real numbers.

Notes:

Extra Practice

In Exercises 1–4, rewrite the equation in exponential form.

1. $\log_{10} 1000 = 3$ 2. $\log_5 \dfrac{1}{25} = -2$ 3. $\log_{10} 1 = 0$ 4. $\log_{1/4} 64 = -3$

Name_____ Date _____

In Exercises 5–8, rewrite the equation in logarithmic form.

5. $12^2 = 144$ **6.** $20^{-1} = \dfrac{1}{20}$ **7.** $216^{1/3} = 6$ **8.** $4^0 = 1$

In Exercises 9–12, evaluate the logarithm.

9. $\log_4 64$ **10.** $\log_{1/8} 1$ **11.** $\log_2 \dfrac{1}{32}$ **12.** $\log_{1/25} \dfrac{1}{5}$

In Exercises 13 and 14, simplify the expression.

13. $13^{\log_{13} 6}$ **14.** $\ln e^{x^3}$

In Exercises 15 and 16, find the inverse of the function.

15. $y = 15^x + 10$ **16.** $y = \ln(2x) - 8$

In Exercises 17 and 18, graph the function. Determine the asymptote of the function.

17. $y = \log_2(x + 1)$ **18.** $y = \log_{1/2} x - 4$

5.3 Transformations of Exponential and Logarithmic Functions
For use with Exploration 5.3

Essential Question How can you transform the graphs of exponential and logarithmic functions?

1 EXPLORATION: Identifying Transformations

Work with a partner. Each graph shown is a transformation of the parent function

$$f(x) = e^x \qquad \text{or} \qquad f(x) = \ln x.$$

Match each function with its graph. Explain your reasoning. Then describe the transformation of f represented by g.

a. $g(x) = e^{x+2} - 3$ **b.** $g(x) = -e^{x+2} + 1$ **c.** $g(x) = e^{x-2} - 1$

d. $g(x) = \ln(x + 2)$ **e.** $g(x) = 2 + \ln x$ **f.** $g(x) = 2 + \ln(-x)$

A.

B.

C.

D.

E.

F.

5.3 **Transformations of Exponential and Logarithmic Functions** (continued)

2 **EXPLORATION:** Characteristics of Graphs

Work with a partner. Determine the domain, range, and asymptote of each function in Exploration 1. Justify your answers.

Communicate Your Answer

3. How can you transform the graphs of exponential and logarithmic functions?

4. Find the inverse of each function in Exploration 1. Then check your answer by using a graphing calculator to graph each function and its inverse in the same viewing window.

Name _____ Date _____

5.3 Notetaking with Vocabulary
For use after Lesson 5.3

In your own words, write the meaning of each vocabulary term.

exponential function

logarithmic function

transformations

Core Concepts

Transformation	$f(x)$ Notation	Examples	
Horizontal Translation Graph shifts left or right.	$f(x - h)$	$g(x) = 4^{x-3}$ $g(x) = 4^{x+2}$	3 units right 2 units left
Vertical Translation Graph shifts up or down.	$f(x) + k$	$g(x) = 4^x + 5$ $g(x) = 4^x - 1$	5 units up 1 unit down
Reflection Graph flips over x- or y-axis.	$f(-x)$ $-f(x)$	$g(x) = 4^{-x}$ $g(x) = -4^x$	in the y-axis in the x-axis
Horizontal Stretch or Shrink Graph stretches away from or shrinks toward y-axis	$f(ax)$	$g(x) = 4^{2x}$ $g(x) = 4^{x/2}$	shrink by a factor of $\frac{1}{2}$ stretch by a factor of 2
Vertical Stretch or Shrink Graph stretches away from or shrinks toward x-axis	$a \bullet f(x)$	$g(x) = 3(4^x)$ $g(x) = \frac{1}{4}(4^x)$	stretch by a factor of 3 shrink by a factor of $\frac{1}{4}$

Notes:

5.3 Notetaking with Vocabulary (continued)

Transformation	$f(x)$ Notation	Examples	
Horizontal Translation Graph shifts left or right.	$f(x - h)$	$g(x) = \log(x - 4)$ $g(x) = \log(x + 7)$	4 units right 7 units left
Vertical Translation Graph shifts up or down.	$f(x) + k$	$g(x) = \log x + 3$ $g(x) = \log x - 1$	3 units up 1 unit down
Reflection Graph flips over x- or y-axis.	$f(-x)$ $-f(x)$	$g(x) = \log(-x)$ $g(x) = -\log x$	in the y-axis in the x-axis
Horizontal Stretch or Shrink Graph stretches away from or shrinks toward y-axis	$f(ax)$	$g(x) = \log(4x)$ $g(x) = \log\left(\frac{1}{3}x\right)$	shrink by a factor of $\frac{1}{4}$ stretch by a factor of 3
Vertical Stretch or Shrink Graph stretches away from or shrinks toward x-axis	$a \bullet f(x)$	$g(x) = 5 \log x$ $g(x) = \frac{2}{3} \log x$	stretch by a factor of 5 shrink by a factor of $\frac{2}{3}$

Notes:

Name _____ Date _____

Extra Practice

In Exercises 1–6, describe the transformation of *f* represented by *g*. Then graph each function.

1. $f(x) = 6^x, g(x) = 6^x + 6$

2. $f(x) = e^x, g(x) = e^{x-4}$

3. $f(x) = \log_5 x, g(x) = \frac{1}{2}\log_5(x + 7)$

4. $f(x) = \log_{1/3} x, g(x) = \log_{1/3} x - \frac{4}{3}$

5. $f(x) = \left(\frac{1}{5}\right)^x, g(x) = \left(\frac{1}{5}\right)^{-3x} + 4$

6. $f(x) = \log x, g(x) = -3\log(x - 2)$

5.4 Properties of Logarithms
For use with Exploration 5.4

Essential Question How can you use properties of exponents to derive properties of logarithms?

Let $x = \log_b m$ and $y = \log_b n$.

The corresponding exponential forms of these two equations are

$b^x = m$ and $b^y = n$.

1 EXPLORATION: Product Property of Logarithms

Work with a partner. To derive the Product Property, multiply m and n to obtain

$mn = b^x b^y = b^{x+y}$.

The corresponding logarithmic form of $mn = b^{x+y}$ is $\log_b mn = x + y$. So,

$\log_b mn = $ _____.   Product Property of Logarithms

2 EXPLORATION: Quotient Property of Logarithms

Work with a partner. To derive the Quotient Property, divide m by n to obtain

$$\frac{m}{n} = \frac{b^x}{b^y} = b^{x-y}.$$

The corresponding logarithmic form of $\frac{m}{n} = b^{x-y}$ is $\log_b \frac{m}{n} = x - y$. So,

$\log_b \frac{m}{n} = $ _____.   Quotient Property of Logarithms

3 EXPLORATION: Power Property of Logarithms

Work with a partner. To derive the Power Property, substitute b^x for m in the expression $\log_b m^n$, as follows.

$$\begin{aligned}
\log_b m^n &= \log_b \left(b^x\right)^n && \text{Substitute } b^x \text{ for } m. \\
&= \log_b b^{nx} && \text{Power of a Power Property of Exponents} \\
&= nx && \text{Inverse Property of Logarithms}
\end{aligned}$$

Name_____ Date _____

5.4 **Properties of Logarithms** (continued)

3 **EXPLORATION: Power Property of Logarithms** (continued)

So, substituting $\log_b m$ for x, you have

$$\log_b m^n = \underline{\hspace{1.5cm}}.$$ Power Property of Logarithms

Communicate Your Answer

4. How can you use properties of exponents to derive properties of logarithms?

5. Use the properties of logarithms that you derived in Explorations 1–3 to evaluate each logarithmic expression.

   a. $\log_4 16^3$

   b. $\log_3 81^{-3}$

   c. $\ln e^2 + \ln e^5$

   d. $2 \ln e^6 - \ln e^5$

   e. $\log_5 75 - \log_5 3$

   f. $\log_4 2 + \log_4 32$

Name_____ Date_____

5.4 **Notetaking with Vocabulary**
For use after Lesson 5.4

In your own words, write the meaning of each vocabulary term.

base

properties of exponents

Core Concepts

Properties of Logarithms

Let b, m, and n be positive real numbers with $b \neq 1$.

Product Property $\log_b mn = \log_b m + \log_b n$

Quotient Property $\log_b \dfrac{m}{n} = \log_b m - \log_b n$

Power Property $\log_b m^n = n \log_b m$

Notes:

Change-of-Base Formula

If a, b, and c are positive real numbers with $b \neq 1$ and $c \neq 1$, then

$$\log_c a = \frac{\log_b a}{\log_b c}.$$

In particular, $\log_c a = \dfrac{\log a}{\log c}$ and $\log_c a = \dfrac{\ln a}{\ln c}$.

Notes:

5.4 Notetaking with Vocabulary (continued)

Extra Practice

In Exercises 1–4, use $\log_2 5 \approx 2.322$ and $\log_2 12 \approx 3.585$ to evaluate the logarithm.

1. $\log_2 60$

2. $\log_2 \dfrac{1}{144}$

3. $\log_2 \dfrac{12}{25}$

4. $\log_2 720$

In Exercises 5–8, expand the logarithmic expression.

5. $\log 10x$

6. $\ln 2x^6$

7. $\log_3 \dfrac{x^4}{3y^3}$

8. $\ln \sqrt[4]{3y^2}$

In Exercises 9–13, condense the logarithmic expression.

9. $\log_2 3 + \log_2 8$

10. $\log_5 4 - 2\log_5 5$

11. $3\ln 6x + \ln 4y$

12. $\log_2 625 - \log_2 125 + \dfrac{1}{3}\log_2 27$

13. $-\log_6 6 - \log_6 2y + 2\log_6 3x$

Name_____ Date _____

5.4 Notetaking with Vocabulary (continued)

In Exercises 14–17, use the change-of-base formula to evaluate the logarithm.

14. $\log_3 17$ **15.** $\log_9 294$ **16.** $\log_7 \frac{4}{9}$ **17.** $\log_6 \frac{1}{10}$

18. For a sound with intensity I (in watts per square meter), the loudness $L(I)$ of the sound (in decibels) is given by the function $L(I) = 10 \log \dfrac{I}{I_0}$, where I_0 is the intensity of a barely audible sound (about 10^{-12} watts per square meter). The intensity of the sound of a certain children's television show is half the intensity of the adult show that is on before it. By how many decibels does the loudness decrease?

19. Hick's Law states that given n equally probable choices, such as choices on a menu, the average human's reaction time T (in seconds) required to choose from those choices is approximately $T = a + b \bullet \log_2(n + 1)$ where a and b are constants. If $a = 4$ and $b = 1$, how much longer would it take a customer to choose what to eat from a menu of 40 items than from a menu of 10 items?

5.5 Solving Exponential and Logarithmic Equations
For use with Exploration 5.5

Essential Question How can you solve exponential and logarithmic equations?

> **1 EXPLORATION:** Solving Exponential and Logarithmic Equations

Work with a partner. Match each equation with the graph of its related system of equations. Explain your reasoning. Then use the graph to solve the equation.

a. $e^x = 2$ 　　　　　　　　　　　　　**b.** $\ln x = -1$

c. $2^x = 3^{-x}$ 　　　　　　　　　　　**d.** $\log_4 x = 1$

e. $\log_5 x = \dfrac{1}{2}$ 　　　　　　　　**f.** $4^x = 2$

A. 　　　　　**B.**

C. 　　　　　**D.**

E. 　　　　　**F.**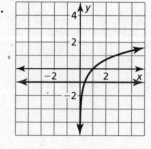

5.5 Solving Exponential and Logarithmic Equations (continued)

---

2 EXPLORATION: Solving Exponential and Logarithmic Equations

Go to _BigIdeasMath.com_ for an interactive tool to investigate this exploration.

Work with a partner. Look back at the equations in Explorations 1(a) and 1(b). Suppose you want a more accurate way to solve the equations than using a graphical approach.

a. Show how you could use a *numerical approach* by creating a table. For instance, you might use a spreadsheet to solve the equations.

b. Show how you could use an *analytical approach*. For instance, you might try solving the equations by using the inverse properties of exponents and logarithms.

Communicate Your Answer

3. How can you solve exponential and logarithmic equations?

4. Solve each equation using any method. Explain your choice of method.

a. $16^x = 2$

b. $2^x = 4^{2x+1}$

c. $2^x = 3^{x+1}$

d. $\log x = \dfrac{1}{2}$

e. $\ln x = 2$

f. $\log_3 x = \dfrac{3}{2}$

5.5 Notetaking with Vocabulary
For use after Lesson 5.5

In your own words, write the meaning of each vocabulary term.

exponential equations

logarithmic equations

Core Concepts

Property of Equality for Exponential Equations

Algebra   If b is a positive real number other than 1, then $b^x = b^y$ if and only if $x = y$.

Example   If $3^x = 3^5$, then $x = 5$. If $x = 5$, then $3^x = 3^5$.

Notes:

Property of Equality for Logarithmic Equations

Algebra   If b, x, and y are positive real numbers with $b \neq 1$, then $\log_b x = \log_b y$ if and only if $x = y$.

Example   If $\log_2 x = \log_2 7$, then $x = 7$. If $x = 7$, then $\log_2 x = \log_2 7$.

Notes:

5.5 **Notetaking with Vocabulary** (continued)

Extra Practice

In Exercises 1–6, solve the equation.

1. $2^{2x+4} = 2^{5x-8}$

2. $4^{2x-1} = 8^{x+2}$

3. $3^{x+3} = 5$

4. $\left(\dfrac{1}{5}\right)^{3x-2} = \sqrt{25^x}$

5. $12e^{1-x} = 500$

6. $-14 + 3e^x = 11$

In Exercises 7–11, solve the equation. Check for extraneous solutions.

7. $2 = \log_3(4x)$

8. $\ln(x^2 + 3) = \ln(4)$

9. $\log_8(x^2 - 5) = \dfrac{2}{3}$

10. $\ln x + \ln(x + 2) = \ln(x + 6)$

11. $\log_2(x + 5) - \log_2(x - 2) = 3$

12. Solve the inequality $\log x \le \dfrac{1}{2}$.

13. Your parents buy juice for your graduation party and leave it in their hot car. When they take the cans out of the car and move them to the basement, the temperature of the juice is 80°F. The room temperature of the basement is 60°F, and the cooling rate of the juice is $r = 0.0147$. Using Newton's Law of Cooling, how long will it take to cool the juice to 63°F?

14. Earthquake intensity is measured by the formula $R = \log\left(\dfrac{I}{I_0}\right)$ where R is the Richter scale rating of an earthquake, I is the intensity of the earthquake, and I_0 is the intensity of the smallest detectable wave. In 1906, an earthquake in San Francisco had an estimated measure of 7.8 on the Richter scale. In the same year, another earthquake had an intensity level four times stronger than the San Francisco earthquake giving it a Richter scale rating of $R_2 = \log\left(\dfrac{4I}{I_0}\right)$. What was the Richter scale rating on a scale of 1–10 of the other earthquake?

5.6 Modeling with Exponential and Logarithmic Functions
For use with Exploration 5.6

Essential Question How can you recognize polynomial, exponential, and logarithmic models?

1 EXPLORATION: Recognizing Different Types of Models

Go to *BigIdeasMath.com* for an interactive tool to investigate this exploration.

Work with a partner. Match each type of model with the appropriate scatter plot. Use a regression program to find a model that fits the scatter plot.

  a. linear (positive slope) **b.** linear (negative slope) **c.** quadratic

  d. cubic   **e.** exponential   **f.** logarithmic

A.

B.

C.

D.

E.

F.

5.6 **Modeling with Exponential and Logarithmic Functions** (continued)

2 **EXPLORATION:** Exploring Gaussian and Logistic Models

Go to *BigIdeasMath.com* for an interactive tool to investigate this exploration.

Work with a partner. Two common types of functions that are related to exponential functions are given. Use a graphing calculator to graph each function. Then determine the domain, range, intercept, and asymptote(s) of the function.

a. Gaussian Function: $f(x) = e^{-x^2}$ b. Logistic Function: $f(x) = \dfrac{1}{1 + e^{-x}}$

Communicate Your Answer

3. How can you recognize polynomial, exponential, and logarithmic models?

4. Use the Internet or some other reference to find real-life data that can be modeled using one of the types given in Exploration 1. Create a table and a scatter plot of the data. Then use a regression program to find a model that fits the data.

Name_____ Date_____

Notetaking with Vocabulary
For use after Lesson 5.6

In your own words, write the meaning of each vocabulary term.

finite differences

common ratio

point-slope form

Notes:

Name_____ Date _____

5.6 **Notetaking with Vocabulary** (continued)

Extra Practice

In Exercises 1 and 2, determine the type of function represented by the table.
Explain your reasoning.

1.

x	6	7	8	9	10	11
y	34	47	62	79	98	119

2.

x	−5	−3	−1	1	3	5
y	$\frac{1}{5}$	$\frac{3}{5}$	$\frac{9}{5}$	$\frac{27}{5}$	$\frac{81}{5}$	$\frac{243}{5}$

In Exercises 3–6, write an exponential function $y = ab^x$ whose graph passes
through the given points.

3. $(1, 12), (3, 108)$

4. $(-1, 2), (3, 32)$

5. $(2, 9), (4, 324)$

6. $(-2, 2), (1, 0.25)$

5.6 **Notetaking with Vocabulary** (continued)

7. An Olympic swimmer starts selling a new type of goggles. The table shows the number y of goggles sold during a 6-month period.

Months, x	1	2	3	4	5	6
Goggles sold, y	28	47	64	79	97	107

   a. Create a scatterplot of the data.

   b. Create a scatterplot of the data pairs $(x, \ln y)$ to show that an exponential model should be a good fit for the original data pairs (x, y). Write a function that models the data.

   c. Use a graphing calculator to write an exponential model for the data.

   d. Use each model to predict the number of goggles sold after 1 year.

Chapter 6 Maintaining Mathematical Proficiency

Evaluate.

1. $\dfrac{2}{3} + \dfrac{2}{3}$

2. $\dfrac{1}{5} + \dfrac{1}{4}$

3. $-\dfrac{5}{6} + \dfrac{3}{4}$

4. $\dfrac{9}{11} - \dfrac{2}{11}$

5. $\dfrac{1}{5} - \dfrac{7}{10}$

6. $\dfrac{5}{8} - \dfrac{1}{6}$

7. $-\dfrac{3}{8} + \dfrac{2}{9} - \dfrac{1}{2}$

8. $\dfrac{3}{4} - \left(-\dfrac{1}{8}\right)$

9. $\dfrac{13}{18} + \dfrac{2}{9} - \dfrac{1}{2}$

Simplify.

10. $\dfrac{\frac{2}{3}}{\frac{8}{15}}$

11. $\dfrac{\frac{1}{6}}{-\frac{2}{3}}$

12. $\dfrac{\frac{3}{4}}{12}$

13. $\dfrac{1}{\frac{1}{5} + \frac{2}{5}}$

14. $\dfrac{2}{\frac{4}{9} - \frac{2}{3}}$

15. $\dfrac{\frac{1}{2} + \frac{1}{5}}{\frac{7}{10} - \frac{2}{5}}$

6.1 Inverse Variation
For use with Exploration 6.1

Essential Question How can you recognize when two quantities vary directly or inversely?

---

1 **EXPLORATION:** Recognizing Direct Variation

Go to *BigIdeasMath.com* for an interactive tool to investigate this exploration.

Work with a partner. You hang different weights from the same spring.

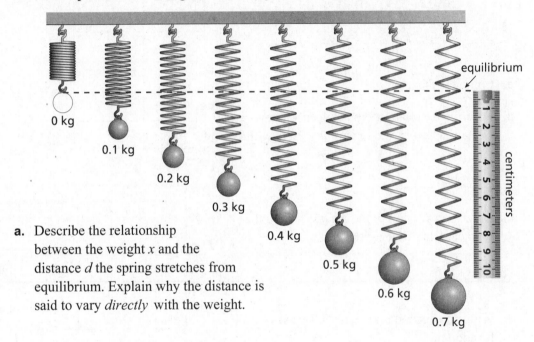

0 kg
0.1 kg
0.2 kg
0.3 kg
0.4 kg
0.5 kg
0.6 kg
0.7 kg
equilibrium
centimeters

a. Describe the relationship between the weight x and the distance d the spring stretches from equilibrium. Explain why the distance is said to vary *directly* with the weight.

b. Estimate the values of d from the figure. Then draw a scatter plot of the data. What are the characteristics of the graph?

c. Write an equation that represents d as a function of x.

d. In physics, the relationship between d and x is described by *Hooke's Law*. How would you describe Hooke's Law?

6.1 Inverse Variation (continued)

2 **EXPLORATION:** Recognizing Inverse Variation

Go to *BigIdeasMath.com* for an interactive tool to investigate this exploration.

Work with a partner. The table shows the length x (in inches) and the width y (in inches) of a rectangle. The area of each rectangle is 64 square inches.

y 64 in.^{2}

x

x	y
1	
2	
4	
8	
16	
32	
64	

   a. Complete the table.

   b. Describe the relationship between x and y. Explain why y is said to vary *inversely* with x.

   c. Draw a scatter plot of the data. What are the characteristics of the graph?

   d. Write an equation that represents y as a function of x.

Communicate Your Answer

   3. How can you recognize when two quantities vary directly or inversely?

   4. Does the flapping rate of the wings of a bird vary directly or inversely with the length of its wings? Explain your reasoning.

6.1 Notetaking with Vocabulary
For use after Lesson 6.1

In your own words, write the meaning of each vocabulary term.

inverse variation

constant of variation

Core Concepts

Inverse Variation

Two variables x and y show **inverse variation** when they are related as follows:

$$y = \frac{a}{x}, \; a \neq 0$$

The constant a is the **constant of variation,** and y is said to *vary inversely* with x.

Notes:

6.1 **Notetaking with Vocabulary** (continued)

Extra Practice

In Exercises 1–9, tell whether *x* and *y* show *direct variation*, *inverse variation*, or *neither*.

1. $3xy = 1$

2. $\dfrac{5}{x} = y$

3. $x + 11 = y$

4. $x + y = -2$

5. $\dfrac{4}{5}x = y$

6. $x - 8y = 1$

7. $\dfrac{x}{7} = y$

8. $6xy = 0$

9. $\dfrac{y}{9x} = 1$

In Exercises 10–12, tell whether *x* and *y* show *direct variation*, *inverse variation*, or *neither*.

10.

x	2	4	6	8	10
y	4	16	36	64	100

11.

x	1	5	8	20	50
y	5	1	0.625	0.25	0.1

12.

x	2	5	8.4	12	15
y	0.5	1.25	2.1	3	3.75

6.1   **Notetaking with Vocabulary** (continued)

In Exercises 13–16, the variables x and y vary inversely. Use the given values to write an equation relating x and y. Then find y when $x = 5$.

13. $x = 2,\ y = 2$

14. $x = 6,\ y = 3$

15. $x = 20,\ y = \dfrac{7}{20}$

16. $x = \dfrac{10}{9},\ y = \dfrac{3}{2}$

17. When temperature is held constant, the volume V of a gas is inversely proportional to the pressure P of the gas on its container. A pressure of 32 pounds per square inch results in a volume of 20 cubic feet. What is the pressure if the volume becomes 10 cubic feet?

18. The time t (in days) that it takes to harvest a field varies inversely with the number n of farm workers. A farmer can harvest his crop in 20 days with 7 farm workers. How long will it take to harvest the crop if he hires 10 farm workers?

6.2 Graphing Rational Functions
For use with Exploration 6.2

Essential Question What are some of the characteristics of the graph of a rational function?

The parent function for rational functions with a linear numerator and a linear denominator is

$$f(x) = \frac{1}{x}. \qquad \text{Parent function}$$

The graph of this function, shown at the right, is a *hyperbola*.

1 EXPLORATION: Identifying Graphs of Rational Functions

Work with a partner. Each function is a transformation of the graph of the parent function $f(x) = \frac{1}{x}$. Match the function with its graph. Explain your reasoning. Then describe the transformation.

a. $g(x) = \dfrac{1}{x-1}$

b. $g(x) = \dfrac{-1}{x-1}$

c. $g(x) = \dfrac{x+1}{x-1}$

d. $g(x) = \dfrac{x-2}{x+1}$

e. $g(x) = \dfrac{x}{x+2}$

f. $g(x) = \dfrac{-x}{x+2}$

A.

B.

6.2 **Graphing Rational Functions** (continued)

---

1 **EXPLORATION:** Identifying Graphs of Rational Functions (continued)

C.

D.

E.

F.

Communicate Your Answer

2. What are some of the characteristics of the graph of a rational function?

3. Determine the intercepts, asymptotes, domain, and range of the rational function

$$g(x) = \frac{x - a}{x - b}.$$

6.2 Notetaking with Vocabulary
For use after Lesson 6.2

In your own words, write the meaning of each vocabulary term.

rational function

Core Concepts

Parent Function for Simple Rational Functions

The graph of the parent function $f(x) = \dfrac{1}{x}$ is a *hyperbola*,

which consists of two symmetrical parts called branches. The domain and range are all nonzero real numbers.

Any function of the form $g(x) = \dfrac{a}{x} (a \neq 0)$ has the same

asymptotes, domain, and range as the function $f(x) = \dfrac{1}{x}$.

Notes:

6.2 **Notetaking with Vocabulary** (continued)

Graphing Translations of Simple Rational Functions

To graph a rational function of the form $y = \dfrac{a}{x - h} + k$, follow these steps:

Step 1 Draw the asymptotes $x = h$ and $y = k$.

Step 2 Plot points to the left and to the right of the vertical asymptote.

Step 3 Draw the two branches of the hyperbola so that they pass through the plotted points and approach the asymptotes.

Notes:

Extra Practice

In Exercises 1 and 2, graph the function. Compare the graph with the graph of $f(x) = \dfrac{1}{x}$.

1. $g(x) = \dfrac{0.25}{x}$

2. $h(x) = \dfrac{-2}{x}$

6.2 **Notetaking with Vocabulary** (continued)

In Exercises 3 and 4, graph the function. State the domain and range.

3. $k(x) = \dfrac{1}{x - 3} + 5$

4. $m(x) = \dfrac{-3}{x} - 4$

In Exercises 5 and 6, rewrite the function in the form $g(x) = \dfrac{a}{x - h} + k$. **Graph the function. Describe the graph of** g **as a transformation of the graph of** $f(x) = \dfrac{a}{x}$.

5. $g(x) = \dfrac{x + 2}{x - 5}$

6. $g(x) = \dfrac{2x + 8}{3x - 12}$

6.3 Multiplying and Dividing Rational Expressions
For use with Exploration 6.3

Essential Question How can you determine the excluded values in a product or quotient of two rational expressions?

---

1 **EXPLORATION:** Multiplying and Dividing Rational Expressions

Work with a partner. Find the product or quotient of the two rational expressions. Then match the product or quotient with its excluded values. Explain your reasoning.

Product or Quotient   **Excluded Values**

a. $\dfrac{1}{x-1} \cdot \dfrac{x-2}{x+1} =$ A. $-1, 0,$ and 2

b. $\dfrac{1}{x-1} \cdot \dfrac{-1}{x-1} =$ B. -2 and 1

c. $\dfrac{1}{x-2} \cdot \dfrac{x-2}{x+1} =$ C. $-2, 0,$ and 1

d. $\dfrac{x+2}{x-1} \cdot \dfrac{-x}{x+2} =$ D. -1 and 2

e. $\dfrac{x}{x+2} \div \dfrac{x+1}{x+2} =$ E. $-1, 0,$ and 1

f. $\dfrac{x}{x-2} \div \dfrac{x+1}{x} =$ F. -1 and 1

g. $\dfrac{x}{x+2} \div \dfrac{x}{x-1} =$ G. -2 and -1

h. $\dfrac{x+2}{x} \div \dfrac{x+1}{x-1} =$ H. 1

6.3 **Multiplying and Dividing Rational Expressions** (continued)

---

2 **EXPLORATION:** Writing a Product or Quotient

Work with a partner. Write a product or quotient of rational expressions that has the given excluded values. Justify your answer.

    a. −1

    b. −1 and 3

    c. −1, 0, and 3

Communicate Your Answer

3. How can you determine the excluded values in a product or quotient of two rational expressions?

4. Is it possible for the product or quotient of two rational expressions to have *no* excluded values? Explain your reasoning. If it is possible, give an example.

6.3 Notetaking with Vocabulary
For use after Lesson 6.3

In your own words, write the meaning of each vocabulary term.

rational expression

simplified form of a rational expression

Core Concepts

Simplifying Rational Expressions

Let a, b, and c be expressions with $b \neq 0$ and $c \neq 0$.

Property $\dfrac{a\cancel{c}}{b\cancel{c}} = \dfrac{a}{b}$ Divide out common factor c.

Examples $\dfrac{15}{65} = \dfrac{3 \cdot \cancel{5}}{13 \cdot \cancel{5}} = \dfrac{3}{13}$ Divide out common factor 5.

$\dfrac{4\cancel{(x+3)}}{(x+3)\cancel{(x+3)}} = \dfrac{4}{x+3}$ Divide out common factor $x + 3$.

Notes:

6.3   **Notetaking with Vocabulary** (continued)

Multiplying Rational Expressions

Let a, b, c, and d be expressions with $b \neq 0$ and $d \neq 0$.

Property $\dfrac{a}{b} \cdot \dfrac{c}{d} = \dfrac{ac}{bd}$ Simplify $\dfrac{ac}{bd}$ if possible.

Example

$$\frac{5x^2}{2xy^2} \cdot \frac{6xy^3}{10y} = \frac{30x^3y^3}{20xy^3} = \frac{\cancel{10} \cdot 3 \cdot \cancel{x} \cdot x^2 \cdot \cancel{y^3}}{\cancel{10} \cdot 2 \cdot \cancel{x} \cdot \cancel{y^3}} = \frac{3x^2}{2}, x \neq 0, y \neq 0$$

Notes:

Dividing Rational Expressions

Let a, b, c, and d be expressions with $b \neq 0$, $c \neq 0$, and $d \neq 0$.

Property $\dfrac{a}{b} \div \dfrac{c}{d} = \dfrac{a}{b} \cdot \dfrac{d}{c} = \dfrac{ad}{bc}$ Simplify $\dfrac{ad}{bc}$ if possible.

Example $\dfrac{7}{x+1} \div \dfrac{x+2}{2x-3} = \dfrac{7}{x+1} \cdot \dfrac{2x-3}{x+2} = \dfrac{7(2x-3)}{(x+1)(x+2)}, x \neq \dfrac{3}{2}$

Notes:

6.3 **Notetaking with Vocabulary** (continued)

Extra Practice

In Exercises 1–4, simplify the expression, if possible.

1. $\dfrac{2x^3 - 8x^2}{6x^2}$

2. $\dfrac{5xy^3 - 2x^2y^2}{x^2y^2}$

3. $\dfrac{x^2 - 5x + 4}{x^2 - 2x + 1}$

4. $\dfrac{x^3 + 3x^2}{x^2 - 5x - 24}$

In Exercises 5–10, find the product or the quotient.

5. $\dfrac{3xy}{xy^2} \bullet \dfrac{y}{2x}$

6. $\dfrac{x + y}{7xy} \div \dfrac{4x}{y}$

7. $\dfrac{x(x + 1)}{x - 2} \div \dfrac{(x + 1)(x - 6)}{(x - 6)(x - 9)}$

8. $\dfrac{x^2 - 2x - 3}{x^2 - 1} \bullet \dfrac{x^2 - 2x - 63}{x^2 + 4x - 21}$

9. $\dfrac{x^2 - 2x}{x + 7} \bullet \dfrac{x^3 + 8}{x^3 - 4x}$

10. $\dfrac{x^2 + 2x - 15}{x^2 - 3x - 40} \div \dfrac{x^2 + 8x - 9}{x^2 + x - 72}$

Name _____ Date _____

6.4 Adding and Subtracting Rational Expressions
For use with Exploration 6.4

Essential Question How can you determine the domain of the sum or difference of two rational expressions?

---

1 EXPLORATION: Adding and Subtracting Rational Expressions

Work with a partner. Find the sum or difference of the two rational expressions. Then match the sum or difference with its domain. Explain your reasoning.

Sum or Difference   **Domain**

a. $\dfrac{1}{x-1}+\dfrac{3}{x-1}=$ A. all real numbers except -2

b. $\dfrac{1}{x-1}+\dfrac{1}{x}=$ B. all real numbers except -1 and 1

c. $\dfrac{1}{x-2}+\dfrac{1}{2-x}=$ C. all real numbers except 1

d. $\dfrac{1}{x-1}+\dfrac{-1}{x+1}=$ D. all real numbers except 0

e. $\dfrac{x}{x+2}-\dfrac{x+1}{2+x}=$ E. all real numbers except -2 and 1

f. $\dfrac{x}{x-2}-\dfrac{x+1}{x}=$ F. all real numbers except 0 and 1

g. $\dfrac{x}{x+2}-\dfrac{x}{x-1}=$ G. all real numbers except 2

h. $\dfrac{x+2}{x}-\dfrac{x+1}{x}=$ H. all real numbers except 0 and 2

6.4 **Adding and Subtracting Rational Expressions** (continued)

2 **EXPLORATION:** Writing a Sum or Difference

Work with a partner. Write a sum or difference of rational expressions that has the given domain. Justify your answer.

    a. all real numbers except -1

    b. all real numbers except -1 and 3

    c. all real numbers except -1, 0, and 3

Communicate Your Answer

    3. How can you determine the domain of the sum or difference of two rational expressions?

    4. Your friend found a sum as follows. Describe and correct the error(s).

$$\frac{x}{x+4} + \frac{3}{x-4} = \frac{x+3}{2x}$$

Name _____ Date _____

Notetaking with Vocabulary
For use after Lesson 6.4

In your own words, write the meaning of each vocabulary term.

complex fraction

Core Concepts

Adding or Subtracting with Like Denominators

Let a, b, and c be expressions with $c \neq 0$.

Addition

$$\frac{a}{c} + \frac{b}{c} = \frac{a+b}{c}$$

Subtraction

$$\frac{a}{c} - \frac{b}{c} = \frac{a-b}{c}$$

Notes:

Adding or Subtracting with Unlike Denominators

Let a, b, c, and d be expressions with $c \neq 0$ and $d \neq 0$.

Addition

$$\frac{a}{c} + \frac{b}{d} = \frac{ad}{cd} + \frac{bc}{cd} = \frac{ad+bc}{cd}$$

Subtraction

$$\frac{a}{c} - \frac{b}{d} = \frac{ad}{cd} - \frac{bc}{cd} = \frac{ad-bc}{cd}$$

Notes:

6.4 **Notetaking with Vocabulary** (continued)

Simplifying Complex Fractions

Method 1   If necessary, simplify the numerator and denominator by writing each as a single fraction. Then divide by multiplying the numerator by the reciprocal of the denominator.

Method 2   Multiply the numerator and the denominator by the LCD of *every* fraction in the numerator and denominator. Then simplify.

Notes:

Extra Practice

In Exercises 1–4, find the sum or difference.

1. $\dfrac{1}{x-1} - \dfrac{5}{x-1}$

2. $\dfrac{4x}{3x-5} + \dfrac{x}{3x-5}$

3. $\dfrac{6x}{x+4} + \dfrac{24}{x+4}$

4. $\dfrac{2x^2}{x-7} - \dfrac{14x}{x-7}$

6.4 Notetaking with Vocabulary (continued)

In Exercises 5–7, find the least common multiple of the expressions.

5. $9x^3, 3x^2 - 21x$ **6.** $x + 5, 2x^2 + 11x + 5$ **7.** $x^2 + 5x + 6, x^2 - 3x - 18$

In Exercises 8–11, find the sum or the difference.

8. $\dfrac{3}{2x} + \dfrac{11}{5x}$

9. $\dfrac{15}{x - 2} + \dfrac{3}{x + 8}$

10. $\dfrac{3x}{2x + 1} + \dfrac{10}{2x^2 - 5x - 3}$

11. $\dfrac{x}{x - 7} - \dfrac{2}{x + 1} - \dfrac{8x}{x^2 - 6x - 7}$

In Exercises 12 and 13, simplify the complex fraction.

12. $\dfrac{\dfrac{x}{10} - 3}{5 + \dfrac{1}{x}}$

13. $\dfrac{\dfrac{12}{x^2 - 7x - 44}}{\dfrac{2}{x - 11} + \dfrac{1}{x + 4}}$

6.5 Solving Rational Equations
For use with Exploration 6.5

Essential Question How can you solve a rational equation?

---

1 **EXPLORATION:** Solving Rational Equations

Work with a partner. Match each equation with the graph of its related system of equations. Explain your reasoning. Then use the graph to solve the equation.

a. $\dfrac{2}{x-1} = 1$

b. $\dfrac{2}{x-2} = 2$

c. $\dfrac{-x-1}{x-3} = x+1$

d. $\dfrac{2}{x-1} = x$

e. $\dfrac{1}{x} = \dfrac{-1}{x-2}$

f. $\dfrac{1}{x} = x^2$

A.

B.

C.

D.

E.

F.

6.5 **Solving Rational Equations** (continued)

2 EXPLORATION: Solving Rational Equations

Go to *BigIdeasMath.com* **for an interactive tool to investigate this exploration.**

Work with a partner. Look back at the equations in Explorations 1(d) and 1(e). Suppose you want a more accurate way to solve the equations than using a graphical approach.

a. Show how you could use a *numerical approach* by creating a table. For instance, you might use a spreadsheet to solve the equations.

b. Show how you could use an *analytical approach*. For instance, you might use the method you used to solve proportions.

Communicate Your Answer

3. How can you solve a rational equation?

4. Use the method in either Exploration 1 or 2 to solve each equation.

a. $\dfrac{x+1}{x-1} = \dfrac{x-1}{x+1}$
   b. $\dfrac{1}{x+1} = \dfrac{1}{x^2+1}$
   c. $\dfrac{1}{x^2-1} = \dfrac{1}{x-1}$

6.5 Notetaking with Vocabulary
For use after Lesson 6.5

In your own words, write the meaning of each vocabulary term.

cross multiplying

Notes:

6.5 Notetaking with Vocabulary (continued)

Extra Practice

In Exercises 1–4, solve the equation by cross multiplying. Check your solution(s).

1. $\dfrac{2}{x+8} = \dfrac{5}{2x-7}$

2. $\dfrac{x}{x+1} = \dfrac{-4}{x}$

3. $\dfrac{x+1}{x-3} = \dfrac{x+2}{x-6}$

4. $\dfrac{-2}{x-3} = \dfrac{x+9}{x+21}$

In Exercises 5–12, solve the equation by using the LCD. Check your solution(s).

5. $\dfrac{4}{7} - \dfrac{1}{x} = 6$

6. $\dfrac{3}{x+1} + \dfrac{4}{x+2} = \dfrac{15}{x+2}$

7. $\dfrac{12}{x+4} - \dfrac{7}{x} = \dfrac{22}{x^2+4x}$

8. $3 - \dfrac{18}{x-1} = -\dfrac{12}{x}$

Name_____ Date_____

9. $\dfrac{2}{x-5} + \dfrac{3}{x} = \dfrac{10}{x^2 - 5x}$

10. $\dfrac{x+6}{x-4} - \dfrac{30}{x^2 - 5x + 4} = \dfrac{3}{x-1}$

11. $\dfrac{x}{x-5} + \dfrac{2}{x+2} = \dfrac{11}{x^2 - 3x - 10}$

12. $\dfrac{x-2}{x-4} - \dfrac{2}{x-1} = \dfrac{12}{x^2 - 5x + 4}$

In Exercises 13 and 14, determine whether the inverse of *f* is a function. Then find the inverse.

13. $f(x) = \dfrac{8}{x-3}$

14. $f(x) = \dfrac{12}{x} + 9$

15. You can complete the yard work at your friend's home in 5 hours. Working together, you and your friend can complete the yard work in 3 hours. How long would it take your friend to complete the yard work when working alone?

Let *t* be the time (in hours) your friend would take to complete the yard work when working alone.

	Work Rate	Time	Work Done
You	$\dfrac{1 \text{ yard}}{5 \text{ hours}}$	3 hours	
Friend		3 hours	

Chapter 7   Maintaining Mathematical Proficiency

Complete the table to evaluate the function.

1. $y = 4 + 2^x$

x	y
1	
2	
3	

2. $y = 2x^3 - 5$

x	y
0	
1	
2	

3. $y = -2x + 10$

x	y
-4	
-2	
0	

Solve the equation. Check your solution(s).

4. $50 = 4 + 2x$

5. $\dfrac{1}{3} = 3\left(\dfrac{1}{3}\right)^x$

6. $45 = 5(2x - 1)$

7. $3^x + 12 = 93$

8. $\dfrac{2}{5}x + 8 = 2$

9. $\dfrac{32}{125} = 25\left(\dfrac{2}{5}\right)^x$

Name_____ Date_____

Defining and Using Sequences and Series

For use with Exploration 7.1

Essential Question How can you write a rule for the nth term of a sequence?

A **sequence** is an ordered list of numbers. There can be a limited number or an infinite number of *terms* of a sequence.

$$a_1, a_2, a_3, a_4, ..., a_n, ...$$ Terms of a sequence

Here is an example.

$$1, 4, 7, 10, ..., 3n - 2, ...$$

1 EXPLORATION: Writing Rules for Sequences

Work with a partner. Match each sequence with its graph on the next page. The horizontal axes represent n, the position of each term in the sequence. Then write a rule for the nth term of the sequence, and use the rule to find a_{10}.

a. $1, 2.5, 4, 5.5, 7, ...$ **b.** $8, 6.5, 5, 3.5, 2, ...$ **c.** $\dfrac{1}{4}, \dfrac{4}{4}, \dfrac{9}{4}, \dfrac{16}{4}, \dfrac{25}{4}, ...$

d. $\dfrac{25}{4}, \dfrac{16}{4}, \dfrac{9}{4}, \dfrac{4}{4}, \dfrac{1}{4}, ...$ **e.** $\dfrac{1}{2}, 1, 2, 4, 8, ...$ **f.** $8, 4, 2, 1, \dfrac{1}{2}, ...$

7.1 **Defining and Using Sequences and Series** (continued)

1 **EXPLORATION:** Writing Rules for Sequences (continued)

A.

B.

C.

D.

E.

F.

Communicate Your Answer

2. How can you write a rule for the nth term of a sequence?

3. What do you notice about the relationship between the terms in (a) an arithmetic sequence and (b) a geometric sequence? Justify your answers.

Name_____ Date_____

 Notetaking with Vocabulary
For use after Lesson 7.1

In your own words, write the meaning of each vocabulary term.

sequence

terms of a sequence

series

summation notation

sigma notation

Core Concepts

Sequences

A **sequence** is an ordered list of numbers. A *finite sequence* is a function that has a limited number of terms and whose domain is the finite set $\{1, 2, 3, \ldots, n\}$. The values in the range are called the **terms** of the sequence.

Domain:	1	2	3	4	$\ldots$	n	Relative position of each term
	$\downarrow$	$\downarrow$	$\downarrow$	$\downarrow$		$\downarrow$	
Range:	a_1	a_2	a_3	a_4	$\ldots$	a_n	Terms of the sequence

An *infinite sequence* is a function that continues without stopping and whose domain is the set of positive integers. Here are examples of a finite sequence and an infinite sequence.

Finite sequence: 2, 4, 6, 8   **Infinite sequence:**   2, 4, 6, 8, …

A sequence can be specified by an equation, or *rule*. For example, both sequences above can be described by the rule $a_n = 2n$ or $f(n) = 2n$.

Notes:

7.1 **Notetaking with Vocabulary** (continued)

Series and Summation Notation

When the terms of a sequence are added together, the resulting expression is a **series**. A series can be finite or infinite.

Finite series: $2 + 4 + 6 + 8$

Infinite series: $2 + 4 + 6 + 8 + \cdots$

You can use **summation notation** to write a series. For example, the two series above can be written in summation notation as follows:

Finite series: $2 + 4 + 6 + 8 = \displaystyle\sum_{i=1}^{4} 2i$

Infinite series: $2 + 4 + 6 + 8 + \cdots = \displaystyle\sum_{i=1}^{\infty} 2i$

For both series, the *index of summation* is i and the *lower limit of summation* is 1. The *upper limit of summation* is 4 for the finite series and ∞ (infinity) for the infinite series. Summation notation is also called **sigma notation** because it uses the uppercase Greek letter *sigma*, written $\sum$.

Notes:

Formulas for Special Series

Sum of n terms of 1: $\displaystyle\sum_{i=1}^{n} 1 = n$

Sum of first n positive integers: $\displaystyle\sum_{i=1}^{n} i = \dfrac{n(n+1)}{2}$

Sum of squares of first n positive integers: $\displaystyle\sum_{i=1}^{n} i^2 = \dfrac{n(n+1)(2n+1)}{6}$

Notes:

7.1 Notetaking with Vocabulary (continued)

Extra Practice

In Exercises 1 and 2, write the first six terms of the sequence.

1. $a_n = n^3 - 1$

2. $f(n) = (-2)^{n-1}$

In Exercises 3 and 4, describe the pattern, write the next term, and write a rule for the nth term of the sequence.

3. $-3, -1, 1, 3, \ldots$

4. $\dfrac{2}{5}, \dfrac{4}{5}, \dfrac{6}{5}, \dfrac{8}{5}, \ldots$

5. Write the series $-1 + 4 - 9 + 16 - 25 + \cdots$ using summation notation.

In Exercises 6 and 7, find the sum.

6. $\displaystyle\sum_{n=2}^{5} \dfrac{n}{n-1}$

7. $\displaystyle\sum_{i=1}^{18} i^2$

Analyzing Arithmetic Sequences and Series
For use with Exploration 7.2

Essential Question How can you recognize an arithmetic sequence from its graph?

In an **arithmetic sequence**, the difference of consecutive terms, called the *common difference*, is constant. For example, in the arithmetic sequence 1, 4, 7, 10, . . . , the common difference is 3.

 EXPLORATION: Recognizing Graphs of Arithmetic Sequences

Go to *BigIdeasMath.com* **for an interactive tool to investigate this exploration.**

Work with a partner. Determine whether each graph shows an arithmetic sequence. If it does, then write a rule for the nth term of the sequence, and use a spreadsheet to find the sum of the first 20 terms. What do you notice about the graph of an arithmetic sequence?

a.

b.

c.

d.

7.2 Analyzing Arithmetic Sequences and Series (continued)

---

2 EXPLORATION: Finding the Sum of an Arithmetic Sequence

Work with a partner. A teacher of German mathematician Carl Friedrich Gauss (1777–1855) asked him to find the sum of all the whole numbers from 1 through 100. To the astonishment of his teacher, Gauss came up with the answer after only a few moments. Here is what Gauss did:

$$1 + 2 + 3 + \cdots + 100$$
$$100 + 99 + 98 + \cdots + 1$$
$$\overline{101 + 101 + 101 + \cdots + 101}$$

$$\frac{100 \times 101}{2} = 5050$$

Explain Gauss's thought process. Then write a formula for the sum S_n of the first n terms of an arithmetic sequence. Verify your formula by finding the sums of the first 20 terms of the arithmetic sequences in Exploration 1. Compare your answers to those you obtained using a spreadsheet.

Communicate Your Answer

3. How can you recognize an arithmetic sequence from its graph?

4. Find the sum of the terms of each arithmetic sequence.

   a. $1, 4, 7, 10, \ldots, 301$

   b. $1, 2, 3, 4, \ldots, 1000$

   c. $2, 4, 6, 8, \ldots, 800$

7.2 Notetaking with Vocabulary
For use after Lesson 7.2

In your own words, write the meaning of each vocabulary term.

arithmetic sequence

common difference

arithmetic series

Core Concepts

Rule for an Arithmetic Sequence

Algebra   The nth term of an arithmetic sequence with first term a_1 and common difference d is given by:

$$a_n = a_1 + (n - 1)d$$

Example   The nth term of an arithmetic sequence with a first term of 3 and a common difference of 2 is given by:

$$a_n = 3 + (n - 1)2, \text{ or } a_n = 2n + 1$$

Notes:

The Sum of a Finite Arithmetic Series

The sum of the first n terms of an arithmetic series is $S_n = n\left(\dfrac{a_1 + a_n}{2}\right)$.

In words, S_n is the mean of the first and nth terms, multiplied by the number of terms.

Notes:

7.2 Notetaking with Vocabulary (continued)

Extra Practice

In Exercises 1–4, tell whether the sequence is arithmetic. Explain your reasoning.

1. $1, 4, 7, 12, 17, \ldots$

2. $26, 23, 20, 17, 14, \ldots$

3. $0.3, 0.5, 0.7, 0.9, 1.1, \ldots$

4. $\dfrac{1}{2}, \dfrac{1}{4}, \dfrac{1}{6}, \dfrac{1}{8}, \dfrac{1}{10}, \ldots$

In Exercises 5–8, write a rule for the nth term of the sequence. Then find a_{20}.

5. $3, 9, 15, 21, \ldots$

6. $8, 3, -2, -7, \ldots$

7. $-1, -\dfrac{1}{2}, 0, \dfrac{1}{2}, \ldots$

8. $0.7, 0.2, -0.3, -0.8, \ldots$

7.2 **Notetaking with Vocabulary** (continued)

9. Write a rule for the nth term of the sequence where $a_{12} = -13$ and $d = -2$. Then graph the first six terms of the sequence.

In Exercises 10 and 11, write a rule for the nth term of the sequence.

10. $a_8 = 59, a_{13} = 99$

11. $a_{18} = -5, a_{27} = -8$

12. Find the sum $\sum\limits_{i=1}^{22} (5 - 2i)$.

7.3 Analyzing Geometric Sequences and Series
For use with Exploration 7.3

Essential Question How can you recognize a geometric sequence from its graph?

In a **geometric sequence**, the ratio of any term to the previous term, called the *common ratio*, is constant. For example, in the geometric sequence 1, 2, 4, 8, . . . , the common ratio is 2.

 1 **EXPLORATION:** Recognizing Graphs of Geometric Sequences

Go to *BigIdeasMath.com* for an interactive tool to investigate this exploration.

Work with a partner. Determine whether each graph shows a geometric sequence. If it does, then write a rule for the *n*th term of the sequence and use a spreadsheet to find the sum of the first 20 terms. What do you notice about the graph of a geometric sequence?

a.

b.

c.

d.

7.3 **Analyzing Geometric Sequences and Series** (continued)

2 **EXPLORATION:** Finding the Sum of a Geometric Sequence

Work with a partner. You can write the nth term of a geometric sequence with first term a_1 and common ratio r as

$$a_n = a_1 r^{n-1}.$$

So, you can write the sum S_n of the first n terms of a geometric sequence as

$$S_n = a_1 + a_1 r + a_1 r^2 + a_1 r^3 + \cdots + a_1 r^{n-1}.$$

Rewrite this formula by finding the difference $S_n - rS_n$ and solving for S_n. Then verify your rewritten formula by finding the sums of the first 20 terms of the geometric sequences in Exploration 1. Compare your answers to those you obtained using a spreadsheet.

Communicate Your Answer

3. How can you recognize a geometric sequence from its graph?

4. Find the sum of the terms of each geometric sequence.

    a. $1, 2, 4, 8, \ldots, 8192$

    b. $0.1, 0.01, 0.001, 0.0001, \ldots, 10^{-10}$

7.3 Notetaking with Vocabulary
For use after Lesson 7.3

In your own words, write the meaning of each vocabulary term.

geometric sequence

common ratio

geometric series

Core Concepts

Rule for a Geometric Sequence

Algebra   The nth term of a geometric sequence with first term a_1 and common
ratio r is given by:

$$a_n = a_1 r^{n-1}$$

Example   The nth term of a geometric sequence with a first term of 2 and a
common ratio of 3 is given by:

$$a_n = 2(3)^{n-1}$$

Notes:

The Sum of a Finite Geometric Series

The sum of the first n terms of a geometric series with common ratio $r \neq 1$ is

$$S_n = a_1 \left(\frac{1 - r^n}{1 - r} \right).$$

Notes:

7.3 Notetaking with Vocabulary (continued)

Extra Practice

In Exercises 1–4, tell whether the sequence is geometric. Explain your reasoning.

1. $4, 12, 36, 108, 324, \ldots$

2. $45, 40, 35, 30, 25, \ldots$

3. $1.3, 7.8, 46.8, 280.8, 1684.8, \ldots$

4. $\dfrac{3}{2}, -\dfrac{3}{4}, \dfrac{3}{8}, -\dfrac{3}{16}, \dfrac{3}{32}, \ldots$

In Exercises 5–8, write a rule for the nth term of the sequence. Then find a_6.

5. $6, 18, 54, 162, \ldots$

6. $3, -6, 12, -24, \ldots$

7. $1, \dfrac{5}{2}, \dfrac{25}{4}, \dfrac{125}{8}, \ldots$

8. $-2.4, -16.8, -117.6, -823.2, \ldots$

7.3 Notetaking with Vocabulary *(continued)*

9. Write a rule for the *n*th term of the sequence where $a_8 = 384$ and $r = 2$. Then graph the first six terms of the sequence.

In Exercises 10 and 11, write a rule for the *n*th term of the geometric sequence.

10. $a_3 = 54, a_6 = 1458$

11. $a_2 = -2, a_5 = \dfrac{2}{125}$

12. Find the sum $\displaystyle\sum_{i=0}^{10} 3\left(\dfrac{3}{2}\right)^{i-1}$.

7.4 Finding Sums of Infinite Geometric Series

For use with Exploration 7.4

Essential Question How can you find the sum of an infinite geometric series?

---

1   **EXPLORATION:** Finding Sums of Infinite Geometric Series

---

Go to *BigIdeasMath.com* **for an interactive tool to investigate this exploration.**

Work with a partner. Enter each geometric series in a spreadsheet. Then use the spreadsheet to determine whether the infinite geometric series has a finite sum. If it does, find the sum. Explain your reasoning. (The figure shows a partially completed spreadsheet for part (a).)

a. $1 + \dfrac{1}{2} + \dfrac{1}{4} + \dfrac{1}{8} + \dfrac{1}{16} + \cdots$

	A	B
1	1	1
2	2	0.5
3	3	0.25
4	4	0.125
5	5	0.0625
6	6	0.03125
7	7	
8	8	
9	9	
10	10	
11	11	
12	12	
13	13	
14	14	
15	15	
16	Sum	

b. $1 + \dfrac{1}{3} + \dfrac{1}{9} + \dfrac{1}{27} + \dfrac{1}{81} + \cdots$

c. $1 + \dfrac{3}{2} + \dfrac{9}{4} + \dfrac{27}{8} + \dfrac{81}{16} + \cdots$

d. $1 + \dfrac{5}{4} + \dfrac{25}{16} + \dfrac{125}{64} + \dfrac{625}{256} + \cdots$

e. $1 + \dfrac{4}{5} + \dfrac{16}{25} + \dfrac{64}{125} + \dfrac{256}{625} + \cdots$

f. $1 + \dfrac{9}{10} + \dfrac{81}{100} + \dfrac{729}{1000} + \dfrac{6561}{10,000} + \cdots$

7.4 **Finding Sums of Infinite Geometric Series** (continued)

---

2 EXPLORATION: Writing a Conjecture

Work with a partner. Look back at the infinite geometric series in Exploration 1. Write a conjecture about how you can determine whether the infinite geometric series

$$a_1 + a_1r + a_1r^2 + a_1r^3 + \cdots$$

has a finite sum.

---

3 EXPLORATION: Writing a Formula

Work with a partner. In Lesson 7.3, you learned that the sum of the first n terms of a geometric series with first term a_1 and common ratio $r \neq 1$ is

$$S_n = a_1\left(\frac{1 - r^n}{1 - r}\right).$$

When an infinite geometric series has a finite sum, what happens to r^n as n increases? Explain your reasoning. Write a formula to find the sum of an infinite geometric series. Then verify your formula by checking the sums you obtained in Exploration 1.

Communicate Your Answer

4. How can you find the sum of an infinite geometric series?

5. Find the sum of each infinite geometric series, if it exists.

    a. $1 + 0.1 + 0.01 + 0.001 + 0.0001 + \cdots$ **b.** $2 + \dfrac{4}{3} + \dfrac{8}{9} + \dfrac{16}{27} + \dfrac{32}{81} + \cdots$

7.4 Notetaking with Vocabulary
For use after Lesson 7.4

In your own words, write the meaning of each vocabulary term.

partial sum

Core Concepts

The Sum of an Infinite Geometric Series

The sum of an infinite geometric series with first term a_1 and common ratio r is given by

$$S = \frac{a_1}{1 - r}$$

provided $|r| < 1$. If $|r| \geq 1$, then the series has no sum.

Notes:

Name _____ Date _____

Extra Practice

In Exercises 1 and 2, consider the infinite geometric series. Find and graph the partial sums S_n for $n = 1, 2, 3, 4,$ and 5. Then describe what happens to S_n as n increases.

1. $\dfrac{1}{4} + \dfrac{1}{6} + \dfrac{1}{9} + \dfrac{2}{27} + \dfrac{4}{81} + \cdots$

2. $3 + \dfrac{3}{5} + \dfrac{3}{25} + \dfrac{3}{125} + \dfrac{3}{625} + \cdots$

7.4 **Notetaking with Vocabulary** (continued)

In Exercises 3–6, find the sum of the infinite geometric series, if it exists.

3. $\displaystyle\sum_{n=1}^{\infty} 6\left(\frac{3}{5}\right)^{n-1}$

4. $\displaystyle\sum_{i=1}^{\infty} \frac{10}{3}\left(\frac{5}{2}\right)^{i-1}$

5. $5 + \dfrac{5}{3} + \dfrac{5}{9} + \dfrac{5}{27} + \cdots$

6. $\dfrac{1}{2} - \dfrac{1}{4} + \dfrac{1}{8} - \dfrac{1}{16} + \cdots$

7. A child pushes a tumbler toy and lets it swing freely. On the first swing, the toy travels 30 centimeters. On each successive swing, the toy travels 75% of the distance of the previous swing. What is the total distance the toy swings?

8. Write 0.121212… as a fraction in simplest form.

Name _____ Date _____

Essential Question How can you define a sequence recursively?

A **recursive rule** gives the beginning term(s) of a sequence and a *recursive equation* that tells how a_n is related to one or more preceding terms.

---

1 EXPLORATION: Evaluating a Recursive Rule

Go to *BigIdeasMath.com* for an interactive tool to investigate this exploration.

Work with a partner. Use each recursive rule and a spreadsheet to write the first six terms of the sequence. Classify the sequence as arithmetic, geometric, or neither. Explain your reasoning. (The figure shows a partially completed spreadsheet for part (a).)

	A	B
1	n	nth Term
2	1	7
3	2	10
4	3	
5	4	
6	5	
7	6	

B2+3

a. $a_1 = 7, a_n = a_{n-1} + 3$

b. $a_1 = 5, a_n = a_{n-1} - 2$

c. $a_1 = 1, a_n = 2a_{n-1}$

d. $a_1 = 1, a_n = \frac{1}{2}(a_{n-1})^2$

e. $a_1 = 3, a_n = a_{n-1} + 1$

f. $a_1 = 4, a_n = \frac{1}{2}a_{n-1} - 1$

g. $a_1 = 4, a_n = \frac{1}{2}a_{n-1}$

h. $a_1 = 4, a_2 = 5, a_n = a_{n-1} + a_{n-2}$

7.5 **Using Recursive Rules with Sequences** (continued)

---

2 **EXPLORATION:** Writing a Recursive Rule

Work with a partner. Write a recursive rule for the sequence. Explain your reasoning.

a. $3, 6, 9, 12, 15, 18, \ldots$ b. $18, 14, 10, 6, 2, -2, \ldots$

c. $3, 6, 12, 24, 48, 96, \ldots$ d. $128, 64, 32, 16, 8, 4, \ldots$

e. $5, 5, 5, 5, 5, 5, \ldots$ f. $1, 1, 2, 3, 5, 8, \ldots$

---

3 **EXPLORATION:** Writing a Recursive Rule

Work with a partner. Write a recursive rule for the sequence whose graph is shown.

a.   b.

Communicate Your Answer

4. How can you define a sequence recursively?

5. Write a recursive rule that is different from those in Explorations 1–3. Write the first six terms of the sequence. Then graph the sequence and classify it as arithmetic, geometric, or neither.

7.5 Notetaking with Vocabulary
For use after Lesson 7.5

In your own words, write the meaning of each vocabulary term.

explicit rule

recursive rule

Core Concepts

Recursive Equations for Arithmetic and Geometric Sequences

Arithmetic Sequence

$$a_n = a_{n-1} + d,$$ where d is the common difference

Geometric Sequence

$$a_n = r \cdot a_{n-1},$$ where r is the common ratio

Notes:

7.5 Notetaking with Vocabulary (continued)

Extra Practice

In Exercises 1 and 2, write the first six terms of the sequence.

1. $a_1 = 2$

  $a_n = a_{n-1} + 5$

2. $f(0) = 1$

  $f(n) = 2f(n-1)$

In Exercises 3–6, write a recursive rule for the sequence.

3. $9, 12, 15, 18, 21, \ldots$

4. $50, 20, 8, \dfrac{16}{5}, \dfrac{32}{25}, \ldots$

5. $3, 4, 1, -3, -4, \ldots$

6. $1, 1, \dfrac{1}{3}, \dfrac{1}{4}, \dfrac{1}{15}, \ldots$

7.5 Notetaking with Vocabulary (continued)

In Exercises 7–10, write a recursive rule for the sequence.

7. $a_n = 5 - 3n$

8. $a_n = 10(-2)^{n-1}$

9. $a_n = -1 + 8n$

10. $a_n = -3\left(\dfrac{3}{4}\right)^{n-1}$

In Exercises 11–14, write an explicit rule for each sequence.

11. $a_1 = -1, a_n = a_{n-1} + 7$

12. $a_1 = 24, a_n = 0.2a_{n-1}$

13. $a_1 = 1, a_n = a_{n-1} - 0.3$

14. $a_1 = -2, a_n = -5a_{n-1}$

Chapter 8   Maintaining Mathematical Proficiency

Graph the function.

1. $f(x) = (x + 3)(x - 2)^2$

2. $f(x) = \frac{1}{2}(x + 1)(x - 4)^2$

3. $f(x) = \frac{1}{4}(x + 2)(x - 1)(x - 3)$

Find the missing side length of the triangle.

4.

8 cm

6 cm

c

5.

b

10 m

26 m

6.

c

5 ft

5 ft

7.

a

1.7 in.

0.8 in.

Name_____ Date_____

Essential Question How can you find a trigonometric function of an acute angle θ?

Consider one of the acute angles θ of a right triangle. Ratios of a right triangle's side lengths are used to define the six *trigonometric functions*, as shown.

Sine	$\sin \theta = \dfrac{\text{opp.}}{\text{hyp.}}$	**Cosine**	$\cos \theta = \dfrac{\text{adj.}}{\text{hyp.}}$	
Tangent	$\tan \theta = \dfrac{\text{opp.}}{\text{adj.}}$	**Cotangent**	$\cot \theta = \dfrac{\text{adj.}}{\text{opp.}}$	
Secant	$\sec \theta = \dfrac{\text{hyp.}}{\text{adj.}}$	**Cosecant**	$\csc \theta = \dfrac{\text{hyp.}}{\text{opp.}}$	

---

1 EXPLORATION: Trigonometric Functions of Special Angles

Work with a partner. Find the exact values of the sine, cosine, and tangent functions for the angles 30°, 45°, and 60° in the right triangles shown.

8.1 **Right Triangle Trigonometry** (continued)

2 **EXPLORATION:** Exploring Trigonometric Identities

Work with a partner.

Use the definitions of the trigonometric functions to explain why each *trigonometric identity* is true.

a. $\sin \theta = \cos(90° - \theta)$

b. $\cos \theta = \sin(90° - \theta)$

c. $\sin \theta = \dfrac{1}{\csc \theta}$

d. $\tan \theta = \dfrac{1}{\cot \theta}$

Use the definitions of the trigonometric functions to complete each trigonometric identity.

e. $(\sin \theta)^2 + (\cos \theta)^2 = $ _____

f. $(\sec \theta)^2 - (\tan \theta)^2 = $ _____

Communicate Your Answer

3. How can you find a trigonometric function of an acute angle θ?

4. Use a calculator to find the lengths x and y of the legs of the right triangle shown.

Name_____ Date_____

Notetaking with Vocabulary
For use after Lesson 8.1

In your own words, write the meaning of each vocabulary term.

sine

cosine

tangent

cosecant

secant

cotangent

Core Concepts

Right Triangle Definitions of Trigonometric Functions

Let θ be an acute angle of a right triangle. The six trigonometric functions of θ are defined as shown.

$$\sin \theta = \frac{\text{opposite}}{\text{hypotenuse}} \qquad \cos \theta = \frac{\text{adjacent}}{\text{hypotenuse}} \qquad \tan \theta = \frac{\text{opposite}}{\text{adjacent}}$$

$$\csc \theta = \frac{\text{hypotenuse}}{\text{opposite}} \qquad \sec \theta = \frac{\text{hypotenuse}}{\text{adjacent}} \qquad \cot \theta = \frac{\text{adjacent}}{\text{opposite}}$$

The abbreviations *opp.*, *adj.*, and *hyp.* are often used to represent the side lengths of the right triangle. Note that the ratios in the second row are reciprocals of the ratios in the first row.

$$\csc \theta = \frac{1}{\sin \theta} \qquad \sec \theta = \frac{1}{\cos \theta} \qquad \cot \theta = \frac{1}{\tan \theta}$$

Notes:

8.1   **Notetaking with Vocabulary (continued)**

Trigonometric Values for Special Angles

The table gives the values of the six trigonometric functions for the angles 30°, 45°, and 60°. You can obtain these values from the triangles shown.

θ	$\sin \theta$	$\cos \theta$	$\tan \theta$	$\csc \theta$	$\sec \theta$	$\cot \theta$
30°	$\dfrac{1}{2}$	$\dfrac{\sqrt{3}}{2}$	$\dfrac{\sqrt{3}}{3}$	2	$\dfrac{2\sqrt{3}}{3}$	$\sqrt{3}$
45°	$\dfrac{\sqrt{2}}{2}$	$\dfrac{\sqrt{2}}{2}$	1	$\sqrt{2}$	$\sqrt{2}$	1
60°	$\dfrac{\sqrt{3}}{2}$	$\dfrac{1}{2}$	$\sqrt{3}$	$\dfrac{2\sqrt{3}}{3}$	2	$\dfrac{\sqrt{3}}{3}$

Notes:

Name_____ Date_____

Extra Practice

In Exercises 1 and 2, evaluate the six trigonometric functions of the angle θ.

1.

2.

In Exercises 3 and 4, let θ be an acute angle of a right triangle. Evaluate the other five trigonometric functions of θ.

3. $\tan \theta = 1$

4. $\sin \theta = \dfrac{3}{19}$

In Exercises 5 and 6, find the value of x for the right triangle.

5.

6.

8.2 Angles and Radian Measure
For use with Exploration 8.2

Essential Question How can you find the measure of an angle in radians?

Let the vertex of an angle be at the origin, with one side of the angle on the positive *x*-axis. The *radian measure* of the angle is a measure of the intercepted arc length on a circle of radius 1. To convert between degree and radian measure, use the fact that $\dfrac{\pi \text{ radians}}{180°} = 1$.

---

1 EXPLORATION: Writing Radian Measures of Angles

Work with a partner. Write the radian measure of each angle with the given degree measure. Explain your reasoning.

a.

b.

8.2 **Angles and Radian Measure** (continued)

2 **EXPLORATION: Writing Degree Measures of Angles**

Work with a partner. Write the degree measure of each angle with the given radian measure. Explain your reasoning.

Communicate Your Answer

3. How can you find the measure of an angle in radians?

4. The figure shows an angle whose measure is 30 radians. What is the measure of the angle in degrees? How many times greater is 30 radians than 30 degrees? Justify your answers.

8.2 Notetaking with Vocabulary
For use after Lesson 8.2

In your own words, write the meaning of each vocabulary term.

initial side

terminal side

standard position

coterminal

radian

sector

central angle

Core Concepts

Angles in Standard Position

In a coordinate plane, an angle can be formed by fixing one ray, called the **initial side**, and rotating the other ray, called the **terminal side**, about the vertex.

An angle is in **standard position** when its vertex is at the origin and its initial side lies on the positive x-axis.

Notes:

8.2   **Notetaking with Vocabulary** (continued)

Converting Between Degrees and Radians

Degrees to radians

Multiply degree measure by

$$\frac{\pi \text{ radians}}{180°}.$$

Radians to degrees

Multiply radian measure by

$$\frac{180°}{\pi \text{ radians}}.$$

Degree and Radian Measures of Special Angles

The diagram shows equivalent degree and radian measures for special angles from 0° to 360° (0 radians to 2π radians).

You may find it helpful to memorize the equivalent degree and radian measures of special angles in the first quadrant and for $90° = \dfrac{\pi}{2}$ radians. All other special angles shown are multiples of theses angles.

Arc Length and Area of a Sector

The arc length s and area A of a sector with radius r and central angle θ (measured in radians) are as follows.

Arc length: $s = r\theta$

Area: $A = \dfrac{1}{2}r^2\theta$

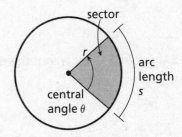

Notes:

8.2 Notetaking with Vocabulary (continued)

Extra Practice

In Exercises 1 and 2, draw an angle with the given measure in standard position.

1. 260°

2. −750°

In Exercises 3–6, find one positive angle and one negative angle that are coterminal with the given angle.

3. 55°

4. −300°

5. 460°

6. −220°

In Exercises 7–10, convert the degree measure to radians or the radian measure to degrees.

7. 54°

8. −310°

9. $\dfrac{16\pi}{15}$

10. $-\dfrac{2\pi}{5}$

8.3 Trigonometric Functions of Any Angle
For use with Exploration 8.3

Essential Question   How can you use the unit circle to define the trigonometric functions of any angle?

Let θ be an angle in standard position with (x, y) a point on the terminal side of θ and $r = \sqrt{x^2 + y^2} \neq 0$. The six trigonometric functions of θ are defined as shown.

$$\sin \theta = \frac{y}{r} \qquad\qquad \csc \theta = \frac{r}{y}, y \neq 0$$

$$\cos \theta = \frac{x}{r} \qquad\qquad \sec \theta = \frac{r}{x}, x \neq 0$$

$$\tan \theta = \frac{y}{x}, x \neq 0 \qquad \cot \theta = \frac{x}{y}, y \neq 0$$

---

1 EXPLORATION: Writing Trigonometric Functions

Work with a partner. Find the sine, cosine, and tangent of the angle θ in standard position whose terminal side intersects the unit circle at the point (x, y) shown.

a. $\left(\dfrac{-1}{2}, \dfrac{\sqrt{3}}{2}\right)$

b. $\left(\dfrac{-1}{\sqrt{2}}, \dfrac{1}{\sqrt{2}}\right)$

c.

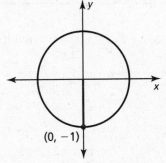

$(0, -1)$

8.3 **Trigonometric Functions of Any Angle** (continued)

1 **EXPLORATION:** Writing Trigonometric Functions (continued)

d.

$\left(\dfrac{1}{2}, \dfrac{-\sqrt{3}}{2}\right)$

e.

$\left(\dfrac{1}{\sqrt{2}}, \dfrac{-1}{\sqrt{2}}\right)$

f.

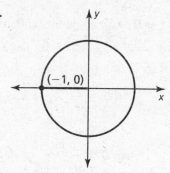

$(-1, 0)$

Communicate Your Answer

2. How can you use the unit circle to define the trigonometric functions of any angle?

3. For which angles are each function undefined? Explain your reasoning.

    a. tangent

    b. cotangent

    c. secant

    d. cosecant

Name_____ Date _____

Notetaking with Vocabulary
For use after Lesson 8.3

In your own words, write the meaning of each vocabulary term.

unit circle

quadrantal angle

reference angle

Core Concepts

General Definitions of Trigonometric Functions

Let θ be an angle in standard position, and let (x, y) be the point where the terminal side of θ intersects the circle $x^2 + y^2 = r^2$. The six trigonometric functions of θ are defined as shown.

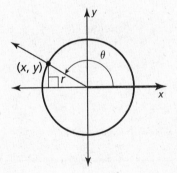

$\sin \theta = \dfrac{y}{r}$ $\qquad$ $\csc \theta = \dfrac{r}{y}, y \neq 0$

$\cos \theta = \dfrac{x}{r}$ $\qquad$ $\sec \theta = \dfrac{r}{x}, x \neq 0$

$\tan \theta = \dfrac{y}{x}, x \neq 0$ $\qquad$ $\cot \theta = \dfrac{x}{y}, y \neq 0$

These functions are sometimes called *circular functions*.

The Unit Circle

The circle $x^2 + y^2 = 1$, which has center $(0, 0)$ and radius 1, is called the **unit circle**. The values of $\sin \theta$ and $\cos \theta$ are simply the y-coordinate and x-coordinate, respectively, of the point where the terminal side of θ intersects the unit circle.

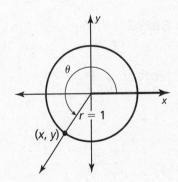

$\sin \theta = \dfrac{y}{r} = \dfrac{y}{1} = y$ $\qquad$ $\cos \theta = \dfrac{x}{r} = \dfrac{x}{1} = x$

Notes:

8.3 **Notetaking with Vocabulary** (continued)

Reference Angle Relationships

Let θ be an angle in standard position. The **reference angle** for θ is the acute angle θ' formed by the terminal side of θ and the x-axis. The relationship between θ and θ' is shown below for nonquadrantal angles θ such that $90° < \theta < 360°$ or, in radians, $\dfrac{\pi}{2} < \theta < 2\pi$.

Quadrant II   **Quadrant III**   **Quadrant IV**

Degrees: $\theta' = 180° - \theta$ Degrees: $\theta' = \theta - 180°$ Degrees: $\theta' = 360° - \theta$

Radians: $\theta' = \pi - \theta$ Radians: $\theta' = \theta - \pi$ Radians: $\theta' = 2\pi - \theta$

Notes:

Evaluating Trigonometric Functions

Use these steps to evaluate a trigonometric function for any angle θ:

Step 1 Find the reference angle θ'.

Step 2 Evaluate the trigonometric function for θ'.

Step 3 Determine the sign of the trigonometric function value from the quadrant in which θ lies.

Signs of Function Values

Quadrant II	Quadrant I
$\sin\theta$, $\csc\theta$: $+$	$\sin\theta$, $\csc\theta$: $+$
$\cos\theta$, $\sec\theta$: $-$	$\cos\theta$, $\sec\theta$: $+$
$\tan\theta$, $\cot\theta$: $-$	$\tan\theta$, $\cot\theta$: $+$
Quadrant III	Quadrant IV
$\sin\theta$, $\csc\theta$: $-$	$\sin\theta$, $\csc\theta$: $-$
$\cos\theta$, $\sec\theta$: $-$	$\cos\theta$, $\sec\theta$: $+$
$\tan\theta$, $\cot\theta$: $+$	$\tan\theta$, $\cot\theta$: $-$

Notes:

Name_____ Date _____

Extra Practice

In Exercises 1 and 2, evaluate the six trigonometric functions of θ.

1.

(2, 6)

θ

2.

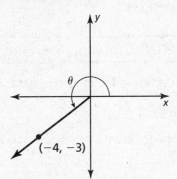

θ

(−4, −3)

In Exercises 3 and 4, use the unit circle to evaluate the six trigonometric functions of θ.

3. $\theta = -90°$

4. $\theta = 4\pi$

In Exercises 5 and 6, sketch the angle. Then find its reference angle.

5. $-310°$

6. $\dfrac{27\pi}{10}$

7. Evaluate the function csc 150° without using a calculator.

8.4 Graphing Sine and Cosine Functions
For use with Exploration 8.4

Essential Question   What are the characteristics of the graphs of the sine and cosine functions?

1   EXPLORATION: Graphing the Sine Function

Go to *BigIdeasMath.com* for an interactive tool to investigate this exploration.

Work with a partner.

a.   Complete the table for $y = \sin x$, where x is an angle measure in radians.

x	-2π	$-\dfrac{7\pi}{4}$	$-\dfrac{3\pi}{2}$	$-\dfrac{5\pi}{4}$	$-\pi$	$-\dfrac{3\pi}{4}$	$-\dfrac{\pi}{2}$	$-\dfrac{\pi}{4}$	0
$y = \sin x$									
x	$\dfrac{\pi}{4}$	$\dfrac{\pi}{2}$	$\dfrac{3\pi}{4}$	π	$\dfrac{5\pi}{4}$	$\dfrac{3\pi}{2}$	$\dfrac{7\pi}{4}$	2π	$\dfrac{9\pi}{4}$
$y = \sin x$									

b.   Plot the points (x, y) from part (a). Draw a smooth curve through the points to sketch the graph of $y = \sin x$.

c.   Use the graph to identify the x-intercepts, the x-values where the local maximums and minimums occur, and the intervals for which the function is increasing or decreasing over $-2\pi \le x \le 2\pi$. Is the sine function *even*, *odd*, or *neither*?

8.4 **Graphing Sine and Cosine Functions** (continued)

2 **EXPLORATION:** Graphing the Cosine Function

Go to *BigIdeasMath.com* for an interactive tool to investigate this exploration.

Work with a partner.

a. Complete the table for $y = \cos x$ using the same values of x as those used in Exploration 1.

x	-2π	$-\dfrac{7\pi}{4}$	$-\dfrac{3\pi}{2}$	$-\dfrac{5\pi}{4}$	$-\pi$	$-\dfrac{3\pi}{4}$	$-\dfrac{\pi}{2}$	$-\dfrac{\pi}{4}$	0
$y = \cos x$									

x	$\dfrac{\pi}{4}$	$\dfrac{\pi}{2}$	$\dfrac{3\pi}{4}$	π	$\dfrac{5\pi}{4}$	$\dfrac{3\pi}{2}$	$\dfrac{7\pi}{4}$	2π	$\dfrac{9\pi}{4}$
$y = \cos x$									

b. Plot the points (x, y) from part (a) and sketch the graph of $y = \cos x$

c. Use the graph to identify the x-intercepts, the x-values where the local maximums and minimums occur, and the intervals for which the function is increasing or decreasing over $-2\pi \le x \le 2\pi$. Is the cosine function *even*, *odd*, or *neither*?

Communicate Your Answer

3. What are the characteristics of the graphs of the sine and cosine functions?

4. Describe the end behavior of the graph of $y = \sin x$.

8.4 Notetaking with Vocabulary
For use after Lesson 8.4

In your own words, write the meaning of each vocabulary term.

amplitude

periodic function

cycle

period

phase shift

midline

Core Concepts

Characteristics of $y = \sin x$ and $y = \cos x$

- The domain of each function is all real numbers.

- The range of each function is $-1 \leq y \leq 1$. So, the minimum value of each function is -1 and the maximum value is 1.

- The **amplitude** of the graph of each function is one-half of the difference of the maximum value and the minimum value, or $\frac{1}{2}\left[1 - (-1)\right] = 1$.

- Each function is **periodic**, which means that its graph has a repeating pattern. The shortest repeating portion of the graph is called a **cycle**. The horizontal length of each cycle is called the **period**. The graph of each function has a period of 2π.

- The x-intercepts for $y = \sin x$ occur when $x = 0, \pm\pi, \pm 2\pi, \pm 3\pi, \ldots$.

- The x-intercepts for $y = \cos x$ occur when $x = \pm\frac{\pi}{2}, \pm\frac{3\pi}{2}, \pm\frac{5\pi}{2}, \pm\frac{7\pi}{2}, \ldots$.

8.4 **Notetaking with Vocabulary** (continued)

Amplitude and Period

The amplitude and period of the graphs of $y = a \sin bx$ and $y = a \cos bx$, where a and b are nonzero real numbers, are as follows:

$$\text{Amplitude} = |a| \qquad\qquad \text{Period} = \frac{2\pi}{|b|}$$

Notes:

Graphing $y = a \sin b(x - h) + k$ and $y = a \cos b(x - h) + k$

To graph $y = a \sin b(x - h) + k$ or $y = a \cos b(x - h) + k$ where $a > 0$ and $b > 0$, follow these steps:

Step 1 Identify the amplitude a, the period $\dfrac{2\pi}{b}$, the horizontal shift h, and the vertical shift k of the graph.

Step 2 Draw the horizontal line $y = k$, called the **midline** of the graph.

Step 3 Find the five key points by translating the key points of $y = a \sin bx$ or $y = a \cos bx$ horizontally h units and vertically k units.

Step 4 Draw the graph through the five translated key points.

Notes:

8.4 Notetaking with Vocabulary (continued)

Extra Practice

In Exercises 1–4, identify the amplitude and period of the function. Then graph the function and describe the graph of g as a transformation of the graph of its parent function.

1. $g(x) = \sin 2x$

2. $g(x) = \dfrac{1}{3} \cos 2x$

3. $g(x) = 4 \sin 2\pi x$

4. $g(x) = \dfrac{1}{2} \cos 3\pi x$

In Exercises 5 and 6, graph the function.

5. $g(x) = \sin \dfrac{1}{2}(x - \pi) + 1$

6. $g(x) = \cos\left(x + \dfrac{\pi}{2}\right) - 3$

8.5 Graphing Other Trigonometric Functions
For use with Exploration 8.5

Essential Question What are the characteristics of the graph of the tangent function?

---

1 EXPLORATION: Graphing the Tangent Function

Go to *BigIdeasMath.com* for an interactive tool to investigate this exploration.

Work with a partner.

a. Complete the table for $y = \tan x$, where x is an angle measure in radians.

x	$-\dfrac{\pi}{2}$	$-\dfrac{\pi}{3}$	$-\dfrac{\pi}{4}$	$-\dfrac{\pi}{6}$	0	$\dfrac{\pi}{6}$	$\dfrac{\pi}{4}$	$\dfrac{\pi}{3}$	$\dfrac{\pi}{2}$
$y = \tan x$									

x	$\dfrac{2\pi}{3}$	$\dfrac{3\pi}{4}$	$\dfrac{5\pi}{6}$	π	$\dfrac{7\pi}{6}$	$\dfrac{5\pi}{4}$	$\dfrac{4\pi}{3}$	$\dfrac{3\pi}{2}$	$\dfrac{5\pi}{3}$
$y = \tan x$									

b. The graph of $y = \tan x$ has vertical asymptotes at x-values where $\tan x$ is undefined. Plot the points (x, y) from part (a). Then use the asymptotes to sketch the graph of $y = \tan x$.

8.5 **Graphing Other Trigonometric Functions** (continued)

1 **EXPLORATION:** Graphing the Tangent Function (continued)

    c. For the graph of $y = \tan x$, identify the asymptotes, the x-intercepts, and the intervals for which the function is increasing or decreasing over $-\dfrac{\pi}{2} \le x \le \dfrac{3\pi}{2}$. Is the tangent function *even*, *odd*, or *neither*?

Communicate Your Answer

    2. What are the characteristics of the graph of the tangent function?

    3. Describe the asymptotes of the graph of $y = \cot x$ on the interval $-\dfrac{\pi}{2} < x < \dfrac{3\pi}{2}$.

8.5 Notetaking with Vocabulary
For use after Lesson 8.5

In your own words, write the meaning of each vocabulary term.

asymptote

period

amplitude

x-intercept

transformations

local maximum

local minimum

Core Concepts

Characteristics of $y = \tan x$ and $y = \cot x$

The functions $y = \tan x$ and $y = \cot x$ have the following characteristics.

- The domain of $y = \tan x$ is all real numbers except odd multiples of $\dfrac{\pi}{2}$. At these x-values, the graph has vertical asymptotes.

- The domain of $y = \cot x$ is all real numbers except multiples of π. At these x-values, the graph has vertical asymptotes.

- The range of each function is all real numbers. So, the functions do not have maximum or minimum values, and the graphs do not have an amplitude.

- The period of each graph is π.

- The x-intercepts for $y = \tan x$ occur when $x = 0, \pm\pi, \pm2\pi, \pm3\pi, \ldots$.

- The x-intercepts for $y = \cot x$ occur when $x = \pm\dfrac{\pi}{2}, \pm\dfrac{3\pi}{2}, \pm\dfrac{5\pi}{2}, \pm\dfrac{7\pi}{2}, \ldots$.

Notes:

8.5   **Notetaking with Vocabulary** (continued)

Period and Vertical Asymptotes of $y = a \tan bx$ and $y = a \cot bx$

The period and vertical asymptotes of the graphs of $y = a \tan bx$ and $y = a \cot bx$, where a and b are nonzero real numbers, are as follows.

- The period of the graph of each function is $\dfrac{\pi}{|b|}$.

- The vertical asymptotes for $y = a \tan bx$ occur at odd multiples of $\dfrac{\pi}{2|b|}$.

- The vertical asymptotes for $y = a \cot bx$ occur at multiples of $\dfrac{\pi}{|b|}$.

Notes:

Characteristics of $y = \sec x$ and $y = \csc x$

The functions $y = \sec x$ and $y = \csc x$ have the following characteristics.

- The domain of $y = \sec x$ is all real numbers except odd multiples of $\dfrac{\pi}{2}$. At these x-values, the graph has vertical asymptotes.

- The domain of $y = \csc x$ is all real numbers except multiples of π. At these x-values, the graph has vertical asymptotes.

- The range of each function is $y \le -1$ and $y \ge 1$. So, the graphs do not have an amplitude.

- The period of each graph is 2π.

Notes:

Name_____ Date_____

Extra Practice

In Exercises 1–6, graph one period of the function. Describe the graph of *g* as a transformation of the graph of its parent function.

1. $g(x) = \tan 2x$

2. $g(x) = 2 \cot \frac{1}{2}x$

3. $g(x) = \frac{1}{4} \tan \frac{\pi}{4}x$

4. $g(x) = \frac{1}{2} \cot 3x$

5. $g(x) = 2 \sec 2x$

6. $g(x) = \csc 2\pi x$

8.6   Modeling with Trigonometric Functions
For use with Exploration 8.6

Essential Question   What are the characteristics of the real-life problems that can be modeled by trigonometric functions?

1   **EXPLORATION:** Modeling Electric Currents

> **Work with a partner.** Find a sine function that models the electric current shown in each oscilloscope screen. State the amplitude and period of the graph.

a.

b.

c.

d.

8.6 **Modeling with Trigonometric Functions** (continued)

1 **EXPLORATION: Modeling Electric Currents** (continued)

e.

f.

Communicate Your Answer

2. What are the characteristics of the real-life problems that can be modeled by trigonometric functions?

3. Use the Internet or some other reference to find examples of real-life situations that can be modeled by trigonometric functions.

Name _____ Date _____

In your own words, write the meaning of each vocabulary term.

frequency

sinusoid

Notes:

Name_____ Date _____

Extra Practice

1. An alternating current generator (AC generator) converts motion to electricity by generating sinusoidal voltage. Assuming that there is no vertical offset and phase shift, the voltage oscillates between −170 volts and +170 volts with a frequency of 60 hertz. Write and graph a sine model that gives the voltage V as a function of the time t (in seconds).

In Exercises 2–5, write a function for the sinusoid.

2.

3.

8.6 **Notetaking with Vocabulary** (continued)

4.

5.

6. The pedal of a bicycle wheel is 7 inches long. The lowest point of the pedal is 4 inches above the ground. A cyclist pedals 3 revolutions per second. Write a model for the height h (in inches) of the pedal as a function of the time t (in seconds) given that the pedal is at its lowest point when $t = 0$.

7. The London Eye, the tallest Ferris wheel in Europe, has a diameter of 120 meters and the whole structure is 135 meters tall. The Ferris wheel completes one revolution in about 30 minutes. Write a model for the height h (in meters) of a passenger capsule as a function of the time t (in seconds) given that the capsule is at its highest point when $t = 0$.

Name_____ Date_____

Solve the proportion.

1. $\dfrac{2x - 5}{34} = \dfrac{9}{17}$

2. $\dfrac{7}{25} = \dfrac{14}{8 + 4x}$

3. $\dfrac{24}{3x - 17} = \dfrac{15}{19}$

4. $\dfrac{x}{4} = \dfrac{16}{x}$

Solve △ABC using the diagram and the given measurements.

5. $B = 16°, b = 14$

6. $A = 72°, c = 16$

7. $A = 27°, b = 9$

8. $A = 64°, a = 7.4$

Using Trigonometric Identities
For use with Exploration 9.1

Essential Question How can you verify a trigonometric identity?

 EXPLORATION: Writing a Trigonometric Identity

Work with a partner. In the figure, the points (x, y) is on a circle of radius c with center at the origin.

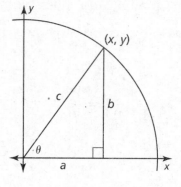

    a. Write an equation that relates a, b, and c.

    b. Write expressions for the sine and cosine ratios of angle θ.

    c. Use the results from parts (a) and (b) to find the sum of $\sin^2\theta$ and $\cos^2\theta$.

    d. Use a table to verify that the identity you wrote in part (c) is valid for angles in each of the four quadrants.

    e. The trigonometric identity you derived in part (c) is called a *Pythagorean identity*. There are two other Pythagorean identities. Divide each side of the identity in part (c) by $\cos^2\theta$ and simplify. Divide each side of the identity in part (c) by $\sin^2\theta$ and simplify.

Name_____ Date_____

2 **EXPLORATION:** Writing Cofunction Identities

Work with a partner. Use the figure at the right. Recall that the two acute angles of a right triangle are complementary. Given the radian measure of one of the acute angles of a right triangle is θ, the measure of the other must be $\dfrac{\pi}{2} - \theta$.

a. Write expressions for the six trigonometric functions of the angle θ and of the angle $\dfrac{\pi}{2} - \theta$.

b. Which expressions in part (a) are equivalent? Use the results to write trigonometric identities for the six trigonometric functions of the angle $\dfrac{\pi}{2} - \theta$.

3 **EXPLORATION:** Writing Negative Angle Identities

Work with a partner. Use the figure at the right.

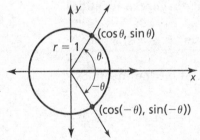

a. Describe the transformation of the point $(\cos \theta, \sin \theta)$ that results from replacing θ with $-\theta$. Explain your reasoning.

b. Use the coordinate rule for the transformation you described in part (a) to write trigonometric identities for $\cos(-\theta)$ and $\sin(-\theta)$.

c. Use the results of part (b) to write trigonometric identities for the remaining four trigonometric functions of the angle $-\theta$.

Communicate Your Answer

4. How can you verify a trigonometric identify?

5. Is $\sin \theta = \cos \theta$ a trigonometric identity? Explain your reasoning.

9.1 Notetaking with Vocabulary
For use after Lesson 9.1

In your own words, write the meaning of each vocabulary term.

trigonometric identity

Core Concepts

Fundamental Trigonometric Identities

Reciprocal Identities

$$\sin \theta = \frac{1}{\csc \theta} \qquad \cos \theta = \frac{1}{\sec \theta} \qquad \tan \theta = \frac{1}{\cot \theta}$$

$$\csc \theta = \frac{1}{\sin \theta} \qquad \sec \theta = \frac{1}{\cos \theta} \qquad \cot \theta = \frac{1}{\tan \theta}$$

Tangent and Cotangent Identities

$$\tan \theta = \frac{\sin \theta}{\cos \theta} \qquad \cot \theta = \frac{\cos \theta}{\sin \theta}$$

Pythagorean Identities

$$\sin^2 \theta + \cos^2 \theta = 1 \qquad 1 + \tan^2 \theta = \sec^2 \theta \qquad 1 + \cot^2 \theta = \csc^2 \theta$$

Cofunction Identities

$$\sin\left(\frac{\pi}{2} - \theta\right) = \cos \theta \qquad \cos\left(\frac{\pi}{2} - \theta\right) = \sin \theta \qquad \tan\left(\frac{\pi}{2} - \theta\right) = \cot \theta$$

$$\csc\left(\frac{\pi}{2} - \theta\right) = \sec \theta \qquad \sec\left(\frac{\pi}{2} - \theta\right) = \csc \theta \qquad \cot\left(\frac{\pi}{2} - \theta\right) = \tan \theta$$

Negative Angle Identities

$$\sin(-\theta) = -\sin \theta \qquad \cos(-\theta) = \cos \theta \qquad \tan(-\theta) = -\tan \theta$$

$$\csc(-\theta) = -\csc \theta \qquad \sec(-\theta) = \sec \theta \qquad \cot(-\theta) = -\cot \theta$$

Notes:

9.1 Notetaking with Vocabulary (continued)

Extra Practice

In Exercises 1–4, find the values of the other five trigonometric functions of θ.

1. $\sin \theta = \dfrac{1}{5}, \dfrac{\pi}{2} < \theta < \pi$

2. $\cos \theta = -\dfrac{4}{5}, \pi < \theta < \dfrac{3\pi}{2}$

3. $\cot \theta = \dfrac{4}{7}, 0 < \theta < \dfrac{\pi}{2}$

4. $\sec \theta = \dfrac{\sqrt{13}}{3}, \dfrac{3\pi}{2} < \theta < 2\pi$

In Exercises 5–8, simplify the expression.

5. $-\dfrac{\tan \theta}{\sec \theta}$

6. $\cos\left(\dfrac{\pi}{2} - \theta\right)\left(1 - \cos^2 \theta\right)$

9.1 Notetaking with Vocabulary (continued)

7. $\dfrac{2\sec^2 x - 2\tan^2 x}{\tan(-x)\,\cos(-x)}$

8. $\dfrac{-\sin\left(\dfrac{\pi}{2} - \theta\right)}{\sec(-\theta)} - \sin^2\theta$

In Exercises 9 and 10, verify the identity.

9. $\dfrac{1 - \cos^2\theta}{\sec^2\theta} - \sin^2\theta = -\sin^4\theta$

10. $\csc x + \cot x = \dfrac{\sin x}{1 - \cos x}$

Name_____ Date_____

9.2 Using Sum and Difference Formulas

For use with Exploration 9.2

Essential Question How can you evaluate trigonometric functions of the sum or difference of two angles?

 EXPLORATION: Deriving a Difference Formula

Work with a partner.

a. Explain why the two triangles shown are congruent.

 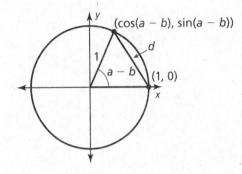

b. Use the Distance Formula to write an expression for d in the first unit circle.

c. Use the Distance Formula to write an expression for d in the second unit circle.

d. Write an equation that relates the expressions in parts (b) and (c). Then simplify this equation to obtain a formula for $\cos(a - b)$.

2 **EXPLORATION:** Deriving a Sum Formula

Work with a partner. Use the difference formula you derived in Exploration 1 to write a formula for $\cos(a + b)$ in terms of sine and cosine of a and b. *Hint:* Use the fact that

$$\cos(a + b) = \cos\big[a - (-b)\big].$$

9.2 **Using Sum and Difference Formulas** (continued)

---

3 **EXPLORATION:** Deriving Difference and Sum Formulas

Work with a partner. Use the formulas you derived in Explorations 1 and 2 to write formulas for $\sin(a - b)$ and $\sin(a + b)$ in terms of sine and cosine of a and b. *Hint*: Use the cofunction identities

$$\sin\left(\frac{\pi}{2} - a\right) = \cos a \text{ and } \cos\left(\frac{\pi}{2} - a\right) = \sin a$$

and the fact that

$$\cos\left[\left(\frac{\pi}{2} - a\right) + b\right] = \sin(a - b) \text{ and } \sin(a + b) = \sin[a - (-b)].$$

Communicate Your Answer

4. How can you evaluate trigonometric functions of the sum or difference of two angles?

5. **a.** Find the exact values of $\sin 75°$ and $\cos 75°$ using sum formulas. Explain your reasoning.

   b. Find the exact values of $\sin 75°$ and $\cos 75°$ using difference formulas. Compare your answers to those in part (a).

Name_____ Date_____

In your own words, write the meaning of each vocabulary term.

ratio

Core Concepts

Sum and Difference Formulas

Sum Formulas	**Difference Formulas**

$\sin(a + b) = \sin a \cos b + \cos a \sin b$ $\qquad$ $\sin(a - b) = \sin a \cos b - \cos a \sin b$

$\cos(a + b) = \cos a \cos b - \sin a \sin b$ $\qquad$ $\cos(a - b) = \cos a \cos b + \sin a \sin b$

$\tan(a + b) = \dfrac{\tan a + \tan b}{1 - \tan a \tan b}$ $\qquad$ $\tan(a - b) = \dfrac{\tan a - \tan b}{1 + \tan a \tan b}$

Notes:

Name _____ Date _____

Extra Practice

In Exercises 1–4, find the exact value of the expression.

1. $\sin(-75°)$

2. $\tan 120°$

3. $\cos\left(-\dfrac{7\pi}{12}\right)$

4. $\cos \dfrac{35\pi}{12}$

In Exercises 5–8, evaluate the expression given that $\sin a = -\dfrac{4}{5}$ with $\pi < a < \dfrac{3\pi}{2}$ and $\cos b = \dfrac{5}{13}$ with $0 < b < \dfrac{\pi}{2}$.

5. $\cos(a - b)$

6. $\sin(a + b)$

9.2 **Notetaking with Vocabulary** (continued)

7. $\tan(a + b)$

8. $\tan(a - b)$

In Exercises 9–12, simplify the expression.

9. $\sin\left(x + \dfrac{\pi}{2}\right)$

10. $\tan(x - 2\pi)$

11. $\cos(x - 2\pi)$

12. $\cos\left(x + \dfrac{5\pi}{2}\right)$

In Exercises 13 and 14, solve the equation for $0 \le x \le 2\pi$.

13. $\sin\left(x + \dfrac{3\pi}{2}\right) = 1$

14. $\sin\left(x - \dfrac{\pi}{2}\right) + \cos\left(x - \dfrac{\pi}{2}\right) = 0$

9.3 Law of Sines
For use with Exploration 9.3

Essential Question   What is the Law of Sines?

1   EXPLORATION: Discovering the Law of Sines

Go to *BigIdeasMath.com* for an interactive tool to investigate this exploration.

Work with a partner.

a. Complete the table for the triangle shown. What can you conclude?

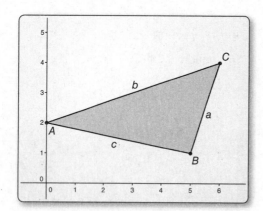

Sample
Segments
$a = 3.16$
$b = 6.32$
$c = 5.10$
Angles
$A = 29.74°$
$B = 97.13°$
$C = 53.13°$

A	a	$\dfrac{\sin A}{a}$	B	b	$\dfrac{\sin B}{b}$	C	c	$\dfrac{\sin C}{c}$

b. Use dynamic geometry software to draw two other triangles. Complete a table
    for each triangle. Use your results to write a conjecture about the relationship
    between the sines of the angles and the lengths of the sides of a triangle.

A	a	$\dfrac{\sin A}{a}$	B	b	$\dfrac{\sin B}{b}$	C	c	$\dfrac{\sin C}{c}$

A	a	$\dfrac{\sin A}{a}$	B	b	$\dfrac{\sin B}{b}$	C	c	$\dfrac{\sin C}{c}$

9.3 **Law of Sines** (continued)

---

2 **EXPLORATION:** Discovering Cases of the Law of Sines

Go to *BigIdeasMath.com* for an interactive tool to investigate this exploration.

Work with a partner.

   a. Begin constructing △*ABC* by drawing side *AC* and acute angle *A*, as shown.

   b. Set a compass to the distance from point *C* to the other side of the angle. How many triangles can you construct using this setting as the length of side *BC*? Explain your reasoning.

   c. Repeat part (b) using a compass setting shorter than the setting in part (b).

   d. Repeat part (b) using a compass setting longer than the setting in part (b).

Communicate Your Answer

   3. What is the Law of Sines?

   4. When would you use the Law of Sines to solve a triangle?

Notetaking with Vocabulary
For use after Lesson 9.3

In your own words, write the meaning of each vocabulary term.

Law of Sines

Core Concepts

Area of a Triangle

The area of any triangle is given by one-half the product of the lengths of two sides times the sine of their included angle. For $\triangle ABC$ shown, there are three ways to calculate the area.

$$\text{Area} = \frac{1}{2}bc \sin A \qquad \text{Area} = \frac{1}{2}ac \sin B \qquad \text{Area} = \frac{1}{2}ab \sin C$$

Notes:

9.3 Notetaking with Vocabulary (continued)

Theorems

Law of Sines

The Law of Sines can be written in either of the following
forms for $\triangle ABC$ with sides of length a, b, and c.

$$\frac{\sin A}{a} = \frac{\sin B}{b} = \frac{\sin C}{c} \qquad\qquad \frac{a}{\sin A} = \frac{b}{\sin B} = \frac{c}{\sin C}$$

Notes:

Possible Triangles in the SSA Case

Consider $\triangle ABC$, where you are given a, b, and A. By fixing side b and angle A, you can
sketch possible positions of side a to figure out how many triangles can be formed. In the
diagram below, note that $h = b \sin A$,

_A_ is obtuse.   **_A_ is acute.**

$a \le b$
No triangle

$h > a$
No triangle

$h = a$
One triangle

$a > b$
One triangle

$h < a < b$
Two triangles

$a \ge b$
One triangle

Notes:

9.3 **Notetaking with Vocabulary** (continued)

Extra Practice

In Exercises 1–3, use a calculator to find the trigonometric ratio. Round your answer to four decimal places.

1. sin 225°

2. cos 111°

3. tan 96°

In Exercises 4 and 5, find the area of the triangle. Round your answer to the nearest tenth.

4.

5.

In Exercises 6–8, solve the triangle. Round decimal answers to the nearest tenth.

6.

7.

8.

Name_____ Date_____

9.4 Law of Cosines
For use with Exploration 9.4

Essential Question What is the Law of Cosines?

1 **EXPLORATION:** Discovering the Law of Cosines

Go to *BigIdeasMath.com* for an interactive tool to investigate this exploration.

Work with a partner.

a. Complete the table for the triangle shown. What can you conclude?

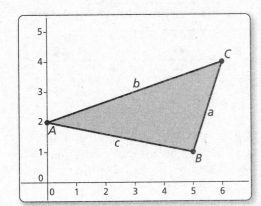

Sample
Segments
$a = 3.16$
$b = 6.32$
$c = 5.10$
Angles
$A = 29.74°$
$B = 97.13°$
$C = 53.13°$

c	c^2	a	a^2	b	b^2	C	$a^2 + b^2 - 2ab \cos C$

b. Use dynamic geometry software to draw two other triangles. Complete a table for each triangle. Use your results to write a conjecture about the relationship between the sines of the angles and the lengths of the sides of a triangle.

c	c^2	a	a^2	b	b^2	C	$a^2 + b^2 - 2ab \cos C$

c	c^2	a	a^2	b	b^2	C	$a^2 + b^2 - 2ab \cos C$

9.4   **Law of Cosines** (continued)

---

2   **EXPLORATION:** Discovering Heron's Area Formula

Go to *BigIdeasMath.com* **for an interactive tool to investigate this exploration.**

Work with a partner.

    a. Complete the table for the triangle in Exploration 1(a). What can you conclude?

a	A	b	c	$s = \frac{1}{2}(a + b + c)$	$\sqrt{s(s - a)(s - b)(s - c)}$	Area $= \frac{1}{2}bc \sin A$

    b. Use dynamic geometry software to draw two other triangles. Complete a table for each triangle. Use your results to write a conjecture about what you observe in the completed tables.

a	A	b	c	$s = \frac{1}{2}(a + b + c)$	$\sqrt{s(s - a)(s - b)(s - c)}$	Area $= \frac{1}{2}bc \sin A$

a	A	b	c	$s = \frac{1}{2}(a + b + c)$	$\sqrt{s(s - a)(s - b)(s - c)}$	Area $= \frac{1}{2}bc \sin A$

Communicate Your Answer

    3. What is the Law of Cosines?

    4. When would you use the Law of Cosines to solve a triangle?

9.4 Notetaking with Vocabulary
For use after Lesson 9.4

In your own words, write the meaning of each vocabulary term.

Law of Cosines

Notes:

Theorems

Law of Cosines

If $\triangle ABC$ has sides of length a, b, and c, as shown, then the following are true.

$$a^2 = b^2 + c^2 - 2bc \cos A$$
$$b^2 = a^2 + c^2 - 2ac \cos B$$
$$c^2 = a^2 + b^2 - 2ab \cos C$$

Notes:

9.4   **Notetaking with Vocabulary** (continued)

Core Concepts

Heron's Area Formula

The area of any triangle with sides of length a, b, and c is

$$\text{Area} = \sqrt{s(s-a)(s-b)(s-c)}$$

Where $s = \frac{1}{2}(a+b+c)$. The variable s is called the *semiperimeter*, or half-perimeter, of the triangle.

Notes:

Extra Practice

In Exercises 1–6, solve $\triangle ABC$. **Round decimal answer to the nearest tenth.**

1.

2.

Name_____ Date_____

3.

4.

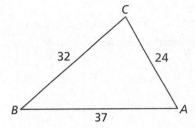

5. $A = 37°, b = 8, c = 11$

6. $a = 5, b = 8, c = 9$

In Exercises 7–9, find the area of $\triangle ABC$. Round your answer to the nearest tenth.

7.

8.

9.

Chapter 10 Maintaining Mathematical Proficiency

Find the mean, median, and mode of the data set. Then determine which measure of center best represents the data. Explain.

1. 26, 24, 55, 21, 32, 26

2. 63, 66, 61, 70, 69, 67, 63, 65

3. 40, 37, 21, 43, 37, 41, 43, 25, 37

Find and interpret the standard deviation of the data set.

4. 18, 11, 15, 20, 16

5. 78, 71, 68, 75, 46, 66

10.1 Using Normal Distributions
For use with Exploration 10.1

Essential Question In a normal distribution, about what percent of the data lies within one, two, and three standard deviations of the mean?

Recall that the standard deviation σ of a numerical data set is given by

$$\sigma = \sqrt{\frac{(x_1 - \mu)^2 + (x_2 - \mu)^2 + \cdots + (x_n - \mu)^2}{n}}$$

where n is the number of values in the data set and μ is the mean of the data set.

---

1 EXPLORATION: Analyzing a Normal Distribution

Work with a partner. In many naturally occurring data sets, the histogram of the data is bell-shaped. In statistics, such data sets are said to have a *normal distribution*. For the normal distribution shown below, estimate the percent of the data that lies within one, two, and three standard deviations of the mean. Each square on the grid represents 1%.

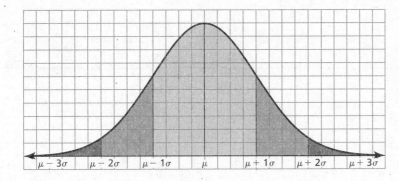

10.1 **Using Normal Distributions** (continued)

2 **EXPLORATION:** Analyzing a Data Set

Work with a partner. A famous data set was collected in Scotland in the mid-1800s. It contains the chest sizes (in inches) of 5738 men in the Scottish Militia. Do the data fit a normal distribution? Explain.

Chest size	Number of men
33	3
34	18
35	81
36	185
37	420
38	749
39	1073
40	1079
41	934
42	658
43	370
44	92
45	50
46	21
47	4
48	1

Communicate Your Answer

3. In a normal distribution, about what percent of the data lies within one, two, and three standard deviations of the mean?

4. Use the Internet or some other reference to find another data set that is normally distributed. Display your data in a histogram.

Name_____ Date_____

In your own words, write the meaning of each vocabulary term.

normal distribution

normal curve

standard normal distribution

z-score

Core Concepts

Areas Under a Normal Curve

A normal distribution with mean μ (the Greek letter mu) and standard deviation σ (the Greek letter sigma) has these properties.

- The total area under the related normal curve is 1.

- About 68% of the area lies within 1 standard deviation of the mean.

- About 95% of the area lies within 2 standard deviations of the mean.

- About 99.7% of the area lies within 3 standard deviations of the mean.

Notes:

10.1 Notetaking with Vocabulary (continued)

Extra Practice

In Exercises 1–6, a normal distribution has mean μ and standard deviation σ. Find the indicated probability for a randomly selected x-value from the distribution.

1. $P(x \le \mu - 2\sigma)$

2. $P(x \ge \mu - 3\sigma)$

3. $P(x \le \mu + 2\sigma)$

4. $P(x \ge \mu + 3\sigma)$

5. $P(\mu - \sigma \le x \le \mu + 3\sigma)$

6. $P(\mu - 2\sigma \le x \le \mu + \sigma)$

7. The scores for a math course test are normally distributed with a mean of 61 and a standard deviation of 11. The test scores range from 0 to 100.

   a. About what percent of the students taking the test have scores between 72 and 83?

   b. About what percent of the students taking the test have scores less than 50?

10.1 **Notetaking with Vocabulary** (continued)

8. The temperatures of a city are normally distributed over the course of a year. The mean temperature is 55.2°F and the standard deviation is 6.3°F. A day is randomly chosen.

   a. What is the probability that the chosen day is 45°F or cooler?

   b. What is the probability that the chosen day is cooler than 32.5°F?

   c. What is the probability that the chosen day is between 32.5°F and 45°F?

   d. What is the probability that the chosen day is 60°F or warmer?

In Exercises 9 and 10, determine whether the histogram has a normal distribution.

9.

10.

10.2 Populations, Samples, and Hypotheses
For use with Exploration 10.2

Essential Question How can you test theoretical probability using sample data?

1 EXPLORATION: Using Sample Data

Go to *BigIdeasMath.com* for an interactive tool to investigate this exploration.

Work with a partner.

    a. When two six-sided dice are rolled, what is the theoretical probability that you roll the same number on both dice?

    b. Conduct an experiment to check your answer in part (a). What sample size did you use? Explain your reasoning.

    c. Use the dice rolling simulator at *BigIdeasMath.com* to complete the table and check your answer to part (a). What happens as you increase the sample size?

Number of Rolls	Number of Times Same Number Appears	Experimental Probability
100		
500		
1000		
5000		
10,000		

2 EXPLORATION: Using Sample Data

Go to *BigIdeasMath.com* for an interactive tool to investigate this exploration.

Work with a partner.

    a. When three six-sided dice are rolled, what is the theoretical probability that you roll the same number on all three dice?

10.2 Populations, Samples, and Hypotheses (continued)

2 **EXPLORATION:** Using Sample Data (continued)

b. Compare the theoretical probability you found in part (a) with the theoretical probability you found in Exploration 1(a).

c. Conduct an experiment to check your answer in part (a). How does adding a die affect the sample size that you use? Explain your reasoning.

d. Use the dice rolling simulator at *BigIdeasMath.com* to check your answer to part (a). What happens as you increase the sample size?

Communicate Your Answer

3. How can you test theoretical probability using sample data?

4. Conduct an experiment to determine the probability of rolling a sum of 7 when two six-sided dice are rolled. Then find the theoretical probability and compare your answers.

10.2 Notetaking with Vocabulary
For use after Lesson 10.2

In your own words, write the meaning of each vocabulary term.

population

sample

parameter

statistic

hypothesis

Notes:

10.2 Notetaking with Vocabulary (continued)

Extra Practice

In Exercises 1–3, identify the population and sample. Describe the sample.

1. In a city, a survey of 3257 adults ages 18 and over found that 2605 of them own a tablet.

2. To find out the consumers' response towards a new flavor of sports drink, a company surveys 1000 athletes who drink sports drinks and finds that 726 of them like the new flavor.

3. In a school district, a survey of 1500 high school students found that 824 of them have a part time job in the summer.

In Exercises 4–7, determine whether the numerical value is a parameter or a statistic. Explain your reasoning.

4. Eighty-two percent of the residents in one neighborhood in a town voted to approve building a bike lane through town.

10.2 **Notetaking with Vocabulary** (continued)

5. In a science class, 25% of the students wear glasses.

6. In a recent year, the median household income in the United States was about $52,000.

7. A survey of some visitors to a museum found that 84% thought the new planetarium was very exciting.

8. You spin the spinner five times and every time the spinner lands on blue. You suspect the spinner favors blue. The maker of the spinner claims that the spinner does not favor any color. You simulate spinning the spinner 50 times by repeatedly drawing 200 random samples of size 50. The histogram shows the results. Use the histogram to determine what you should conclude when you spin the actual spinner 50 times and the spinner lands on blue (a) 12 times and (b) 19 times.

Name_____ Date_____

Essential Question What are some considerations when undertaking a statistical study?

---

1 EXPLORATION: Analyzing Sampling Techniques

Work with a partner. Determine whether each sample is representative of the population. Explain your reasoning.

a. To determine the number of hours people exercise during a week, researchers use random-digit dialing and call 1500 people.

b. To determine how many text messages high school students send in a week, researchers post a survey on a website and receive 750 responses.

c. To determine how much money college students spend on clothes each semester, a researcher surveys 450 college students as they leave the university library.

d. To determine the quality of service customers receive, an airline sends an e-mail survey to each customer after the completion of a flight.

---

2 EXPLORATION: Analyzing Survey Questions

Work with a partner. Determine whether each survey question is biased. Explain your reasoning. If so, suggest an unbiased rewording of the question.

a. Does eating nutritious, whole-grain foods improve your health?

Name_____ Date _____

10.3 Collecting Data (continued)

2 EXPLORATION: Analyzing Survey Questions (continued)

b. Do you ever attempt the dangerous activity of texting while driving?

c. How many hours do you sleep each night?

d. How can the mayor of your city improve his or her public image?

3 EXPLORATION: Analyzing Survey Randomness and Truthfulness

Work with a partner. Discuss each potential problem in obtaining a random survey of a population. Include suggestions for overcoming the problem.

a. The people selected might not be a random sample of the population.

b. The people selected might not be willing to participate in the survey.

c. The people selected might not be truthful when answering the question.

d. The peopled selected might not understand the survey question.

Communicate Your Answer

4. What are some considerations when undertaking a statistical study?

5. Find a real-life example of a biased survey question. Then suggest an unbiased rewording of the question.

Name_____ Date_____

10.3

Notetaking with Vocabulary
For use after Lesson 10.3

In your own words, write the meaning of each vocabulary term.

random sample

self-selected sample

systematic sample

stratified sample

cluster sample

convenience sample

bias

unbiased sample

biased sample

experiment

observational study

survey

10.3 **Notetaking with Vocabulary (continued)**

simulation

biased question

Core Concepts

Types of Samples

For a **self-selected sample**, members of a
population can volunteer to be in the sample.

For a **systematic sample**, a rule is used to
select members of a population. For instance,
selecting every other person.

For a **stratified sample**, a population is divided into smaller groups that share a similar
characteristic. A sample is then randomly selected from each group.

For a **cluster sample**, a population is divided into groups, called *clusters*. All of the members in
one or more of the clusters are selected.

For a **convenience sample**, only members of a population who are easy to reach are selected.

10.3 Notetaking with Vocabulary (continued)

Methods of Collecting Data

An **experiment** imposes a treatment on individuals in order to collect data on their response to the treatment. The treatment may be a medical treatment, or it can be any action that might affect a variable in the experiment, such as adding methanol to gasoline and then measuring its effect on fuel efficiency.

An **observational study** observes individuals and measures variables without controlling the individuals or their environment. This type of study is used when it is difficult to control or isolate the variable being studied, or when it may be unethical to subject people to a certain treatment or to withhold it from them.

A **survey** is an investigation of one or more characteristics of a population. In a survey, every member of a sample is asked one or more questions.

A **simulation** uses a model to reproduce the conditions of a situation or process so that the simulated outcomes closely match the real-world outcomes. Simulations allow you to study situations that are impractical or dangerous to create in real life.

Notes:

Name _____ Date _____

Extra Practice

In Exercises 1–3, identify the type of sample described.

1. A restaurant owner wants to know whether the customers are satisfied with the service. Every fifth customer who exits the restaurant is surveyed.

2. An electronic manufacturer wants to know the customers' responses towards a newly released media player. Emails are sent to customers who recently purchased the device to participate in an online survey at their convenience.

3. A survey is conducted in a state to find out how many households own more than one vehicle. Households are divided into north, east, south, and west regions of the state, and a sample is randomly surveyed from each region.

In Exercises 4 and 5, identify the type of sample and explain why the sample is biased.

4. A manager of a company wants to determine whether the employees are satisfied with the lounge room. The manager surveys the employees who are in the lounge room during lunch break.

5. A news station asks its viewers to participate in an online poll about the presidential candidates.

In Exercises 6 and 7, identify the method of data collection the situation describes.

6. A researcher records whether shoppers at a grocery store buy magazines at the checkout aisles while waiting in line to check out.

7. A meteorologist uses a computer model to track the trajectory of a hurricane.

10.4 Experimental Design
For use with Exploration 10.4

Essential Question How can you use an experiment to test a conjecture?

> **1 EXPLORATION:** Using an Experiment

Work with a partner. Standard white playing dice are manufactured with black dots that are indentations, as shown. So, the side with six indentations is the lightest side and the side with one indentation is the heaviest side.

You make a conjecture that when you roll a standard playing die, the number 6 will come up more often than the number 1 because 6 is the lightest side. To test your conjecture, roll a standard playing die 25 times. Record the results in the table. Does the experiment confirm your conjecture? Explain your reasoning.

lightest side

Number						
Rolls						

10.4 Experimental Design (continued)

2 EXPLORATION: Analyzing an Experiment

Work with a partner. To overcome the imbalance of standard playing dice, one of the authors of this book invented and patented 12-sided dice, on which each number from 1 through 6 appears twice (on opposing sides). See *BigIdeasMath.com*.

As part of the patent process, a standard playing die was rolled 27,090 times. The results are shown below.

Number	1	2	3	4	5	6
Rolls	4293	4524	4492	4397	4623	4761

What can you conclude from the results of this experiment? Explain your reasoning.

Communicate Your Answer

3. How can you use an experiment to test a conjecture?

4. Exploration 2 shows the results of rolling a standard playing die 27,090 times to test the conjecture in Exploration 1. Why do you think the number of trials was so large?

5. Make a conjecture about the outcomes of rolling the 12-sided die in Exploration 2. Then design an experiment that could be used to test your conjecture. Be sure that your experiment is practical to complete and includes enough trials to give meaningful results.

Name_____ Date_____

Notetaking with Vocabulary
For use after Lesson 10.4

In your own words, write the meaning of each vocabulary term.

controlled experiment

control group

treatment group

randomization

randomized comparative experiment

placebo

replication

Core Concepts

Comparative Studies and Causality

- A rigorous randomized comparative experiment, by eliminating sources of variation other than the controlled variable, can make valid cause-and-effect conclusions possible.

- An observational study can identify *correlation* between variables, but not *causality*. Variables, other than what is being measured, may be affecting the results.

Notes:

10.4 Notetaking with Vocabulary (continued)

Extra Practice

In Exercises 1 and 2, determine whether the study is a randomized comparative experiment. If it is, describe the treatment, the treatment group, and the control group. If it is not, explain why not and discuss whether the conclusions drawn from the study are valid.

1.

Baby DVDs

Baby DVDs Improves Language Ability

To test whether baby DVDs that highlight words and introduce music and art can improve language ability, parents with babies 0–24 months were given the choice of whether to let their babies watch the DVDs. Fifty babies who watched the DVDs were observed for a year as well as 50 other babies who did not watch the DVDs. At the end of the year, babies who watched the DVDs scored higher in a language development test.

2.

Type 1 Diabetes

New Drug Improves Blood Glucose Control

In a clinical trial, 100 Type 1 diabetic patients volunteered to take a new drug. Fifty percent of the patients received the drug and the other fifty percent received a placebo. After one year, the patients who received the drug had better blood glucose control while the placebo group experienced no significant change.

10.4 **Notetaking with Vocabulary** (continued)

In Exercises 3 and 4, explain whether the research topic is best investigated through an experiment or an observational study. Then describe the design of the experiment or observational study.

3. A criminologist wants to know whether social factors are the cause of the criminal behavior.

4. A pharmaceutical company wants to know whether the new medication on heart disease has a side effect on individuals.

5. A company wants to test the effectiveness of a new moisturizing cream designed to help improve skin complexion. Identify a potential problem, if any, with each experimental design. Then describe how you can improve it.

   a. The company randomly selects ten individuals. Five subjects are given the new moisturizing cream and the other five are given a placebo. After eight weeks, each subject is evaluated and it is determined that the five subjects who have been using the cream have improved skin complexion.

   b. The company randomly selects a large group of individuals. Half of the individuals are given the new moisturizing cream and the other half of the individuals may use their own existing moisturizers or none at all. After eight weeks, each subject is evaluated and it is determined that a significant large number of subjects who received the moisturizing cream have improved skin complexion.

10.5 Making Inferences from Sample Surveys

For use with Exploration 10.5

Essential Question How can you use a sample survey to infer a conclusion about a population?

---

1 EXPLORATION: Making an Inference from a Sample

Go to *BigIdeasMath.com* for an interactive tool to investigate this exploration.

Work with a partner. You conduct a study to determine what percent of the high school students in your city would prefer an upgraded model of their current cell phone. Based on your intuition and talking with a few acquaintances, you think that 50% of high school students would prefer an upgrade. You survey 50 randomly chosen high school students and find that 20 of them prefer an upgraded model.

50,000 High
School Students

50 Sampled

20 Prefer
Upgrade

a. Based on your sample survey, what percent of the high school students in your city would prefer an upgraded model? Explain your reasoning.

b. In spite of your sample survey, is it still possible that 50% of the high school students in your city prefer an upgraded model? Explain your reasoning.

c. To investigate the likelihood that you could have selected a sample of 50 from a population in which 50% of the population does prefer an upgraded model, you create a binomial distribution as shown below. From the distribution, estimate the probability that exactly 20 students surveyed prefer an upgraded model. Is this event likely to occur? Explain your reasoning.

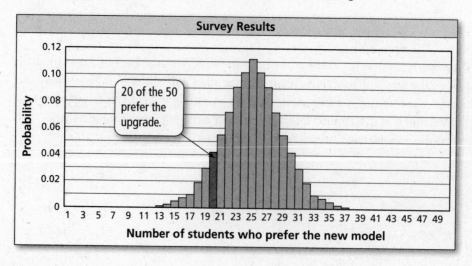

10.5 Making Inferences from Sample Surveys (continued)

1 EXPLORATION: Making an Inference from a Sample (continued)

    d. When making inferences from sample surveys, the sample must be random. In the situation described on the previous page, describe how you could design and conduct a survey using a random sample of 50 high school students who live in a large city.

Communicate Your Answer

    2. How can you use a sample survey to infer a conclusion about a population?

    3. In Exploration 1(c), what is the probability that exactly 25 students you survey prefer an upgraded model?

10.5 Notetaking with Vocabulary
For use after Lesson 10.5

In your own words, write the meaning of each vocabulary term.

descriptive statistics

inferential statistics

margin of error

Core Concepts

Margin of Error Formula

When a random sample of size n is taken from a large population, the margin of error is approximated by

$$\text{Margin of error} = \pm \frac{1}{\sqrt{n}}.$$

This means that if the percent of the sample responding a certain way is p (expressed as a decimal), then the percent of the population who would respond the same way is likely to be between $p - \dfrac{1}{\sqrt{n}}$ and $p + \dfrac{1}{\sqrt{n}}$.

Notes:

10.5 Notetaking with Vocabulary (continued)

Extra Practice

1. The numbers of minutes spent each day on a social networking website by a random sample of people between the ages of 18 and 64 are shown in the table. Estimate the population mean μ.

Number of Minutes				
175	15	190	180	45
100	210	240	190	60
102	165	253	192	102
12	180	189	193	230
300	185	190	395	186
183	200	165	195	409

2. Use the data in Exercise 1 to answer each question.

   a. Estimate the population proportion p of social network users between the ages of 18 and 64 who spend more than 120 minutes each day on a social networking website.

   b. Estimate the population proportion p of social network users between the ages of 18 and 64 who spend fewer than 60 minutes each day on a social networking website.

10.5 **Notetaking with Vocabulary (continued)**

3. Two candidates, A and B, are running for the student council president position. The table shows the results from four surveys of randomly selected students in the school. The students are asked whether they will vote for candidate A. The results are shown in the table.

Sample Size	Number of Votes for Candidate A	Percent of Votes for Candidate A
10	6	60%
20	11	55%
50	20	40%
150	64	42.7%

a. Based on the results of the first two surveys, do you think Candidate A will win the election? Explain.

b. Based on the results in the table, do you think Candidate A will win the election? Explain.

4. A national polling company claims that 39% of Americans rate the overall quality of the environment in the nation as "good." You survey a random sample of 50 people. What can you conclude about the accuracy of the claim that the population proportion is 0.39 when 19 Americans say the quality of the environment is good?

5. In a survey of 2680 people in the U.S., 60% said that their diet is somewhat healthy.

a. What is the margin of error for the survey?

b. Give an interval that is likely to contain the exact percent of all people in the U.S. who think their diet is somewhat healthy.

10.6 Making Inferences from Experiments
For use with Exploration 10.6

Essential Question How can you test a hypothesis about an experiment?

1 **EXPLORATION:** Resampling Data

Go to *BigIdeasMath.com* **for an interactive tool to investigate this exploration.**

Work with a partner. A randomized comparative experiment tests whether water with dissolved calcium affects the yields of yellow squash plants. The table shows the results.

Yield (kilograms)	
Control Group	Treatment Group
1.0	1.1
1.2	1.3
1.5	1.4
0.9	1.2
1.1	1.0
1.4	1.7
0.8	1.8
0.9	1.1
1.3	1.1
1.6	1.8

a. Find the mean yield of the control group and the mean yield of the treatment group. Then find the difference of the two means. Record the results.

b. Write each yield measurement from the table on an equal-sized piece of paper. Place the pieces of paper in a bag, shake, and randomly choose 10 pieces of paper. Call this the "control" group, and call the 10 pieces in the bag the "treatment" group. Then repeat part (a) and return the pieces to the bag. Perform this resampling experiment five times.

c. How does the difference in the means of the control and treatment groups compare with the differences resulting from chance?

10.6   Making Inferences from Experiments (continued)

---

2   EXPLORATION: Evaluating Results

Work as a class. To conclude that the treatment is responsible for the difference in yield, you need strong evidence to reject the hypothesis:

Water dissolved in calcium has no effect on the yields of yellow squash plants.

To evaluate this hypothesis, compare the experimental difference of means with the resampling differences.

    a. Collect all the resampling differences of means found in Exploration 1(b) for the whole class and display these values in a histogram.

    b. Draw a vertical line on your class histogram to represent the experimental difference of means found in Exploration 1(a).

    c. Where on the histogram should the experimental difference of means lie to give evidence for rejecting the hypothesis?

    d. Is your class able to reject the hypothesis? Explain your reasoning.

Communicate Your Answer

3. How can you test a hypothesis about an experiment?

4. The randomized comparative experiment described in Exploration 1 is replicated and the results are shown in the table. Repeat Explorations 1 and 2 using this data set. Explain any differences in your answers.

	Yield (kilograms)								
Control Group	0.9	0.9	1.4	0.6	1.0	1.1	0.7	0.6	1.2	1.3
Treatment Group	1.0	1.2	1.2	1.3	1.0	1.8	1.7	1.2	1.0	1.9

Name_____ Date_____

10.6 Notetaking with Vocabulary
For use after Lesson 10.6

In your own words, write the meaning of each vocabulary term.

randomized comparative experiment

control group

treatment group

mean

dot plot

outlier

simulation

hypothesis

Notes:

10.6 Notetaking with Vocabulary (continued)

Extra Practice

1. A randomized comparative experiment tests whether students who are given weekly
   quizzes do better on the comprehensive final exam. The control group has 10 students
   and the treatment group, which receives weekly quizzes, has 10 students. The table
   shows the results.

	Final Exam Scores (out of 100 points)									
Control Group	82	55	76	92	76	76	82	58	69	79
Treatment Group	92	90	88	73	88	63	94	81	81	77

   a. Find the mean score of the control group.

   b. Find the mean score of the treatment group.

   c. Find the experimental difference of the means.

   d. Display the data in a double dot plot.

   e. What can you conclude?

10.6 Notetaking with Vocabulary (continued)

2. Resample the data in Exercise 1 using a simulation. Use the means of the new control and treatment groups to calculate the difference of the means.

	Final Exam Scores (out of 100 points)								
New Control Group									
New Treatment Group									

3. To analyze the hypothesis below, use the histogram which shows the results from 200 resamplings of the data in Exercise 1.

   Weekly Quizzes have no effect on final exam scores.

   Compare the experimental difference in Exercise 1 with the resampling differences. What can you conclude about the hypothesis? Do weekly quizzes have an effect on final exam scores?

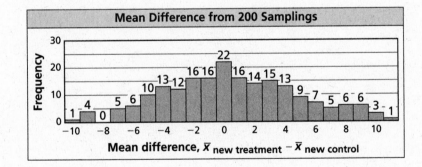